HOPE OVER FEAR

The Promise of Health

⌘

MICOL SANKO

Published by Micol Sanko, Las Vegas, NV 89135.

Cover Design by Katina Desmond
Interior Layout/Graphics by Jean Marie Bauhaus

Printed in the United States of America

ISBN: 978-1-4951-5289-4
ISBN-13: 978-1-4951-5290-0

This book is dedicated to Esha.

She sought help…

She was neglected…

She was treated with ineffective drugs…

She fought to stay, but her life was taken.

Loving Mother, beautiful Sister and caring Wife

A Friend to women,

And a Cancer Warrior through it all!

CONTENTS

ACKNOWLEDGMENTS

Writing this book would not have been possible without the support and encouragement of my close family and friends. I have great gratitude for my editors Natalie Clements & Michael Shuttlesworth who offered their expertise in polishing this manuscript.

⌘

AFFIRMATION

I am made in the perfect image of God. God's light abides within me and thus I carry perfection and intelligence beyond my imagination. I trust completely in this divine light. I ask for healing and I ask to be restored to perfect health. I have asked and I know it is given.

Thank you, thank you, thank you!

If you don't know God's plan for you, seek it in receptive silence.
– Mildred Norman

Steps I Took

Research

- ⌘ Proposed Treatments & Treatment Centers

Surgery, Treatment & Immunotherapy

- ⌘ Radical Hysterectomy,Bilateral Salpingo-Oopherectomy
- ⌘ Tomotherapy
- ⌘ Port Insertion
- ⌘ GTF Chemotherapy with Effective Agents Doxorubicin, Paclitaxel, Irinotecan (per Caris Molecular Intelligence Report) Chelidonine
- ⌘ Neupogen Shots
- ⌘ IV Vitamin C
- ⌘ Oxybosh
- ⌘ PME
- ⌘ Infrared Light Bed
- ⌘ Silver Push
- ⌘ Lymph Flush
- ⌘ Chelation Therapy
- ⌘ Amalgam Filling Removal
- ⌘ Juicing
- ⌘ Coffee Enema
- ⌘ Supplementation & Diet Change

Micol's Treatment Timeline

⌘

PREFACE

IN THE MIDST OF MY BATTLE with aggressive stage IIIB metastatic uterine cancer, I dreamt of this book. Now I offer it, hoping that it will help others who face the difficult task of deciding which treatment path is best for them. In my experience, fear is the oppressive force that insidiously hinders us from choosing the right path. Hope, on the other hand, is the force that has empowered me to overcome my fear. This book is your guide to remaining steadfast in hope and guarded from fear, in your heart, mind, and body.

Because my healing took place in a Christian context, I refer to that belief system. I share each step of my journey because I believe each step was crucial in the miracle of my recovery. I hope you will walk by my side to achieve your own healing, no matter what your belief system.

The process by which we move from illness to health, or sometimes illness to death, may lead us to great human strength, compassion, and ultimately love. Let's beat the odds together. God bless you all.

- *Micol*

⌘

INTRODUCTION

BORN OUT OF A PERSONAL BATTLE with uterine cancer, *Hope Over Fear* offers important information, decision-making exercises, and inspiration to those recently diagnosed with cancer.

Hope Over Fear is your personal guide to making good choices regarding your return to wellness through a blend of facts, memoir, inspiration, and workbook. These combined elements will assist you in making the decision about the path to healing that is right for you.

The integrated format is designed to encourage a well thought out, safe treatment plan of action. This book is intended for easy reading, with each chapter ready to inform, assist, and encourage you. *Hope Over Fear* will bring more clarity and confidence as you make vital decisions regarding your health, and it will help you remain focused during a time that can be extremely overwhelming and stressful. Let the warrior within you emerge, as you trust the directives of your heart and allow yourself to be embraced by faith, hope, and fearlessness.

⌘

NOT STRICKEN?

ACCORDING TO THE AMERICAN Cancer Society 589,430 people will die from cancer in 2015, making it the second most common cause of death in the U.S. The probability of developing cancer in your lifetime in the United States is 43% for men and 38% for women (cancer.org, 2015). These numbers are completely unacceptable.

The absence of illness does not equal health. If you look around, you will find that many people you know are already facing either cancer or some other chronic illness. This means it's time to get on board and start protecting yourself. If you are lucky enough not to have been afflicted yet, this is a great opportunity to utilize your good health for prevention, and protect yourself with a boosted immune system.

Now is also the perfect time to get tested. That is, selective and productive tests which yield valuable information. A list of tests is provided for you in the resource section of this book. It is great preventative medicine to be certain your body is clear of parasites, infections, and toxins, or anything that may compromise your immune system, leaving you vulnerable to illness and cancer.

Through testing, hidden infection or disease will be brought to light and then can be addressed properly. In my opinion, dealing with ailments before they overcome your immune system is essential in the prevention of cancer. Chronic infection, toxicity, parasites, or mold exposure, are all examples of pre-cursers to more difficult health challenges. If you have cancer already, these underlying infections may cause you to lose your battle if they are not addressed. Therefore, it is extremely important they are detected and dealt with from the beginning.

⌘

ROSA

THIS STORY INSPIRED ME, and gave me hope when I was in despair. Rosa was a breast cancer survivor. When she heard of my struggle, she told my husband her story. When Rosa was diagnosed with breast cancer she was in shock and anguish. Shortly afterward, she prayed and felt God telling her she would have to go through all of the treatment but she would feel no side effects. She went on to receive surgery and chemotherapy with absolutely no pain, no side effects, ever.

In the face of my battle, this amazing and inspiring information pushed me to take all preconceived notions and limitations off of the table. Embracing all possibility, I wondered in awe, could I be that blessed? To feel no pain during cancer treatment would be a miracle indeed. Understanding this real life testimonial was an important reminder for me to remain open minded. Letting go of all limitations and imagining the best for my own battle with cancer gave me a profound sense of hope and a strategically powerful mindset.

I share this story as a reminder that anything is possible with your own healing journey. There are no limitations to what can and will happen, except those limitations you hold in your beliefs. Let go of all of your preconceived notions about where this path will lead. If you catch yourself defining your future in any negative way, gently correct yourself and imagine the best possible outcome. Set the stage for your own miracle.

⌘

YOU, THE HOPEFUL BEING

IN MY EXPERIENCE AS A CHRISTIAN, God has been the ultimate positive guiding force in my life. I cannot deny that or my faith in Him. No matter what you call the higher power (inward or outward) in your life, tapping into it is essential to your healing process. In this chapter, and as you know the entire book thus far, I call this power God, the Lord, or the Holy Spirit. I also refer to Jesus. In this book I do not mean to proselytize or convince anyone to change beliefs. By using language I am personally familiar with, I have found I can speak with the most strength and conviction. The divine is universal, no matter what form you believe it takes, if you believe at all. If necessary, substitute any names that appear in this book for a different name that resonates more clearly for you.

Remember God's promise:

You will guard him and keep him in perfect and constant peace whose mind is stayed on You because He commits himself to You, leans on You, and hopes confidently in You.

—Isaiah 26:3 (AMP)

In order to make decisions based on hope and the leading of the Holy Spirit, one must first contemplate what hope really means, then recognize its great power, and finally, celebrate what hope accomplishes on the path to wellness. Today, let us contemplate hope in all of its glory.

What is the definition of hope? Hope is beyond having a positive attitude, beyond simply setting our minds on good things. You could define hope as the feeling that what you wish for can be given. In Hebrews Chapter 11:1 (NIV), we read, "Now faith is confidence in what we hope for and assurance about what we do not see." Based on this scripture, we realize that hopefulness is a form of being faithful.

When we are holding to our faith, we remain hopeful and create room for God's grace to work in our lives. One major obstacle to hopefulness is our limited thinking. Oftentimes we are taught from a very tender age, the "facts of life," some of which are not facts at all. We have learned to think something is either possible or impossible, with nothing beyond this duality. Surely, the answer must be black or white, left or right, yes or no. It is important to recognize those limited beliefs, and let them go. When we limit our own ideas and define what will happen, we may hinder what God can do in our lives. This is not to say we can limit God. As we let go of control, leaving room for greatness, we may receive greater outcomes than what we otherwise might expect.

When considering what hope truly accomplishes, it is indeed a powerful tool. So, what does hope accomplish? Hope overcomes false beliefs and lies. In order to get well, it is important to live in the truth, especially now as you enter the fight for your life. When we are in hopefulness, we leave room for unlimited possibilities. It is this specific aspect of hope that is so powerful and important to remember. Hope, in essence allows us the space where we may coexist with divine grace, which operates within and without ourselves. Hope is a determination in us that we must adhere to:

Let us hold unswervingly to the hope we profess, for he who promised is faithful.

—Hebrews 10:23 (NIV)

In order to make good decisions regarding health, it is necessary to reside in hope. Open yourself up to that space between nothing and everything, leaving room for possibilities beyond limited ideas. Leave despair behind and open up to a world of limitless, unimaginable and beautiful outcomes. The truth that divine intelligence may then reveal to you, the hopeful being.

Take a moment to celebrate the great power of hope. Hope is there for the taking, readily available for you when you choose. Hope defies the most sinister things because it makes us believe that anything can happen. Hope can conquer all fear, dismiss all lies and forget all definition and limitation. Realize that many people, limited by their own perceptions, may speak to you about what they "know" to be true. It is important to recognize that they too are operating under a notion of limitation, oftentimes discounting the reality of unlimited grace, which exists in everyday life. This is why hope is as important as an anecdote to limitation and fearfulness. Hope directs you to believe in all good things.

> *According to your belief, let it be done to you.*
>
> —Matthew 9:29 (NIV)

Let this great, powerful hope be a reminder that God is ever present and ever interested in your life. In your quest for health, let hope lead you in your decision making process. When you make any decision regarding your treatment, always ask yourself, is this a decision that includes hopefulness? A hopeful decision allows for the possibility of greater things than those that are logically apparent. Think upon Psalm 71:14 (ESV) "But I will hope continually, and will praise you yet more and more." Be encouraged and know that to be hopeful is one of the key factors in conquering fear as you face an illness that has been labeled so fierce, so violent, and so unforgiving a killer. Realize that this is only one definition of cancer. Understand that although you are in for a fight for your life, it is *your* fight. You, the hopeful being, have the time and space to be led toward the proper healing path. Pay close attention to the internal knowing that will reveal the way, and do not ignore or resist the divine light of truth that resides in you. Moving toward healing and out of helplessness is your task.

Let hope be your guiding tool, your listening tool, and follow the instructions revealed to you; become obedient in hope. Take a moment now to ask for and receive the restoration of your good health. Ask to receive your miracle, that extraordinary event, a work of God, which is your healing in the physical world. In Christian terms, while you await your miracle realize that nothing is wrong with you because Jesus' blood has been shed for the remission of all your sins.

You are now the righteousness of God in Christ.

—2 Corinthians 5:21

By his one perfect sacrifice, He has perfected you forever.

—Hebrews 10:14

There is no spot in you! You deserve to be blessed. The Holy Spirit knows there is nothing wrong with you, and anyone who says there is has contradicted Him. Say to yourself, I deserve a miracle, and you will receive it.

Now that we know the meaning of hope, we can hold onto it while it works, steadily and powerfully in our lives to annihilate darkness, doubt, and fear. To have hope is to have one of the greatest gifts known to humanity. Acknowledge the power of hope, be steadfast in it, and know that it is your assurance that God will hear you. Expect the return of your birthright, and have faith in your return to wellness!

According to Romans 8:25 (AMP), "But, if we hope for what is still unseen by us, we wait for it with patience and composure." Make a commitment now to listen for answers. This will allow you to hear divine guidance. You will soon read about my healing and I am just like you, the son/daughter of a King. You are also the son or daughter of the great healer and glorious physician. Hope is the foundation of all knowledge and the key to your communication with Him.

Hebrews 6:11 (NASB) declares, "And we desire that each one of you show the same diligence so as to realize the full assurance of hope until the end."

⌘

RESPONSIBILITY & DELEGATION OF CONTROL

TAKE FULL RESPONSIBILITY FOR YOUR own decision-making. Realize that you do have the time it takes to make informed decisions. Do not allow yourself to wither and weaken for fear that your time is limited. Remember, your body is winning right now or else you would not be reading this book. Your body has the power to heal itself. Rise up and become a warrior.

⌘

NO PRAYER GOES UNNOTICED

IT'S LATE AT NIGHT AND I'M lying in bed with the largest smile across my face. I have had a miracle in my life and can't wait to share it. In ecstatic shock, I contemplate what has just occurred.

I have been in Scottsdale, Arizona since the beginning of February, when I began receiving my second round of cancer treatment. The general plan was 24 chemotherapy and 48 radiation sessions. After ten chemo treatments, my doctor became concerned with my dangerously low white blood cell count. I was given a break and received shots to encourage white cell production. At only 112 pounds, my skin turned gray, and I was completely bald. I felt near death, and I didn't see how I could continue with chemo. When I looked in the mirror, I saw an extremely fragile person, who had not one good thing apart from God's grace.

During this reprieve from chemo, an MRI was done. The doctor informed me about my one and a half inch tumor and reminded me he never saw remissions before 21 chemo treatments. I realized I had to find the strength to resume chemo if I wanted to be in remission. I was also due to begin radiation, which had been delayed for several reasons. I had struggled for months at the prospect of accepting radiation as a treatment; indeed, it was one of my greatest fears, and I didn't have confidence in its effectiveness. However, I felt sure it's what God wanted for me.

In the meantime, I was informed of two women who would pray for me. After my friend contacted them, they showed up on a Thursday. One was 80, the other 89 years old. They began to pray over me, and said, "No prayer on my behalf had gone unnoticed." I wept at hearing this truth and a sense of peace came over me. With great dread, I resumed chemo the next day.

On Saturday as I lay in bed, my attention was brought to my abdominal area. I saw an energy sweep across it, and suddenly felt that God revealed to me that the cancer was entirely gone. It was a shock and I thought, could this really be true?

On Monday I told the nurse administering the chemo, "I really believe my cancer has died." She nodded and said, "It could happen." Then, as soon as she pushed the chemo drug in, I felt it swimming in my body with nowhere to go, because the cancer was gone.

My mother arrived that same day. I began to tell her about the women who came to pray over me on Thursday, and how I was sure my cancer had died over the weekend. I knew my immune system was working. I told her how God had assured me and I no longer had any fear of recurrence. She then shared her own story, about how she had been filled with anger and sadness for months at the thought of my suffering and the possibility of losing her daughter and yet, when she landed at the airport and deplaned, all of those terrible feelings lifted, because she knew she was walking into a miracle. We both smiled.

Tuesday morning I decided to reveal what I knew. I said I

would not do any more chemo until I got a PT scan. A PT scan was scheduled for the next morning, and the preliminary result showed the tumor was gone.

My mom said, "You can quit radiation now!" Even though it made logical sense to me, I wanted to wait for the Lord's leading. I asked God for an answer.

At this point I had only completed four out of 48 radiation treatments. At the meeting with my doctor to review my PT scan I was told there was still something called a "hot spot" on the PT scan which could indicate either cancer or healing. I knew it was healing.

I showed up for my fifth radiation appointment only to find that the machine had broken down. After a while, the radiologist returned saying the machine was fixed, and they were going to run my program to check it. Mom said, "This is a God joke." The machine broke again so we left.

I still waited on the Lord for an answer, figuring I would continue until I heard otherwise. The next morning, out of nowhere, I was reminded of the story of Abraham and Isaac in Genesis 22, when God tested Abraham and told him to bring his only son, whom he loved, to the region of Moriah. God said, "Sacrifice him there as a burnt offering on a mountain I will show you." I was reminded that Abraham had been asked by God to do the unthinkable. I was then made aware that even though this was God's request of Abraham, God knew all along that Abraham was not going to have to complete the task!

I took that as my answer. God knew I wouldn't complete all 48 sessions, only four. I was thrilled and amazed at how God had completely released me from the battle with cancer. I could go home with no fear of recurrence, knowing that God wanted my obedience, nothing more. I reflected on my experience during my very last radiation treatment. When I exited the machine for the last time, I felt happy and unafraid. My previous nightmare was in fact a joy in the Lord, who was there with me the entire time.

After quitting radiation, I received frantic calls from the radiologist and was offered more chemo by my doctor, who wanted to be cautious. I told them both that God healed me, told me it would not recur, and that God doesn't take back miracles. I undergo examinations every three months, which have all been clear.

⌘

DO NOT BE SHAKEN

I UNDERSTAND THAT YOU MAY feel overwhelmed right from the start, the point of diagnosis. For this reason I share a bit of my own experience with you and how I made an important choice, one that proved imperative in order to avoid the crippling feeling of becoming overwhelmed.

I was thought to be a person who consistently took good care of myself. I had a better than average diet, and exercised regularly since I was fifteen. I was raised with good health-consciousness. Once while grocery shopping, toting a cart filled with vegetables, my friend commented, "What are you, a rabbit?"

Of course, it came as a shock when a routine ultrasound proved alarming. My OBGYN said, "You may have cancer," after which I sat in a room alone and cried, grieving for my life. I had no idea what I was in for. Stunned and in tears as I walked through the parking lot to my car. I implored God, how could this be? Why me? Why now? What I heard in response was shocking, an immediate reply saying, "It is a gift." I certainly could not imagine what "the gift" in this nightmare could be. In spite of this, I resolved to believe the answer and wait for the gift to be revealed.

Two days later, I was called into the doctor's office and was officially diagnosed with poorly differentiated, or fast moving, aggressive uterine cancer. I was referred to University of Southern California Norris Comprehensive Cancer Center right away to see an oncologist. The doctor at USC told me I would need a radical hysterectomy as soon as possible. The stage would not be known until after the surgery.

I proceeded to tell my close friends and family about my grave condition. In addition to hearing my friends cry, I received an abundance of advice regarding which actions I should take in order to survive, i.e., call a specific office, go to a certain hospital, read this book, take this pill, rush to this doctor or that expert, et cetera, and on and on. All the while, I was extremely ill equipped to do any research, contact any doctors or even think about where to look for solutions as I was in shock, not to mention a deep state of denial, and sheer terror that my life might be over after facing difficult surgeries and treatments.

Naturally, I was completely overwhelmed by the endless possibilities. This led me to contemplate important questions: How does one prepare for death and fight for life at the same time? How does a person process all of the information, proposed treatments, research, and advice? How will I move away from fear and instead achieve great hope, bravery, and courage? How will I overcome this barrage of information and be competent to make extremely important decisions? Answering this particular question seemed critical in order to make life or death decisions while under such duress. I had seen others flounder and rush into decisions for treatment based on fear, and I did not want that for myself. I pondered the countless times I had heard women and men make statements like, "If I had only known there were other options," or, "I wish I would have taken more time and asked more questions." These level-headed people were full of regret because they did not take the time to be sure what they chose was the very best option, one they could trust no matter the outcome, one that would be worth the risk, one that was not based on a belief in fear.

I did not want to get lost in a sea of possibilities, not knowing where to start with the project of saving my own life. I was worried I may be just clueless enough to become disempowered at the prospect of this awesome responsibility.

Faced with this understanding, I realized there was only one imperative and logical decision to make right off the bat: it was vital to choose immediately and ultimately to trust in God. I had to remain filled with hope and faith. I realized that I would be guided through this difficulty, fear, and confusion. I believed if I could make this one choice, this one simple decision, I would be protected from harm. With my faith in God, I knew I would be protected. Within the protected space of hope, I could quiet my mind, relax, let go, and understand that all would be given to me according to my faith.

I can do this, I thought. I decided then to listen for guidance, and trust in the Lord. With this decision I could sort through all of the knowledge, debate, and proposed treatments, while remaining steady in my knowledge that I can do this one thing and I can do it well! Once this decision was made, it became much easier to take care of myself and to fully trust the internal yes' and no's. I could openly listen to people for what resonated as true or right and go from there.

I did not wait for my surgery date to take initiatives such as changing my diet, focusing on positive thoughts and isolating myself so that I could concentrate on my steadfast hopefulness and getting well. I advise you to do the same.

⌘

A PRAYER

I OFFER A PRAYER TO ASSIST you in making the decision to keep your mind on hope during this difficult trial. Feel free to write your own prayer to whomever or whatever you pray to if you are so led.

"Lord, let me begin my assignment from you asking that my faith in you be rooted in hope, and be steadfast and clear. Lord I praise you and ask you to communicate with me, helping me to discern the truth with such clarity that I know what choice to make at every moment. I praise you for giving me the answers and for your promise that once I have asked in Jesus name, it is given to me. I remain quiet and patient as you lead me in light and hope on the right path that glorifies you, and you alone. I acknowledge that I am your son/daughter and that you are my living father that has wonderfully made me, my father who loves me and alights every cell in my body. You have created me and perfected me, in Jesus name I pray, Amen."

When I am overwhelmed, You alone know the way I should turn.

—Psalm 142:3 (NLT)

Trust in the Lord with all your heart and lean not on your own understanding; in all your ways acknowledge Him, and He will direct your paths.

—Proverbs 3:5-6 (KJV)

You created my innermost being; you knit me together in my mother's womb.

—Psalm 139:13

I praise you because I am fearfully and wonderfully made.

—Psalm 139:14 (NIV)

I can do all things through Him who strengthens me.

—Philippians 4:13 (NASV, 1995)

Do not fear, for I am with you; do not anxiously look about you, for I am your God. I will strengthen you, surely I will help you, surely I will uphold you with my righteous right hand.

—Isaiah 41:10 (NASV)

That ye be not soon shaken in mind, or be troubled, neither by spirit, nor by word, nor by letter as from us, as that the day of Christ is at hand.

—Thessalonians 2:22 (KJV)

⌘

FEAR OF HEIGHTS

IT IS THE YEAR 2009 AND I AM in Yosemite with my friend Keena and my husband Carl. We decide to spend the day hiking up the side of a waterfall. I had read that the Park Service did not regularly maintain the trails, railings, and other meaningful safety measures on all hikes. You are basically on your own if you find yourself in peril or have an accident because you had relied on the railings, trails, and other areas to be safe. They have rescues but don't guarantee immediate availability.

My friends know I am terrified of heights. I have not ever been able to overcome the terrible feeling that I will fall whenever I am high up. Therefore Keena, my husband, and I were all cautious in choosing our activities while at Yosemite. Even so, I had noticed on previous days, the hikes we had chosen were not exactly as described in the park literature in terms of the time it took to walk the trails and how difficult they were.

On this particular day, we chose a hike that went up the side of the falls. Before we left, I told my friend Keena that I felt "something big was going to happen." Nevertheless, we proceeded to hike up the falls. While we ascended, the steps became more and more wet with the spray from the falls. As I climbed higher, my breath became more noticeable. I didn't realize until about 20 minutes later that my chest was tightening, and that I was getting anxious, not just breathless. While the grade got steeper, I was on all fours at one point, pulling myself up with my hands while many people were coming down the opposite way.

My focus was at their feet. Some of them carelessly stomped down with great speed onto wet, uneven steps. Many of these people had on sandals. I feared for these people and imagined them falling, which compounded my anxiety.

I finally made it to a point where the stairs ended and there was a small clearing of dirt off to the right, away from the falls. I stood there, relieved I had come to the end, because I was aware I had reached my limit, both physically and emotionally. Before we began the hike, I was told we would not return back the way we had gone initially, and that the return would be easier, going around the top of the waterfall and descending down an easier route. This was the only reason I bore the steps for as long as I did. I loathed the idea of going back down the perilous way we came.

To my dismay, as I looked to the left, all I saw was the vertical face of a rock with a narrow walkway winding around its outside edge, with a shoddy looking railing around it. The walkway actually shot straight out from the face of the rock. Now my focus was on the empty space beneath the path. Nothing supported it, which paralyzed me with fear. Countless people were rushing through, pushing each other while going in both directions on this narrow excuse for a path. I even saw a man with a baby on his back just cruising along as if he were on solid ground, not hovering over what exceeded a 100-foot drop. In sheer terror, I decided there was no way I could continue. Being equally afraid to return the way I had come, I was in a terrible state, spiraling downward, feeling completely out of control. Both my husband and friend tried to calm me, saying I was brave, that I could do this.

I continued plummeting mentally and began to cry uncontrollably. I was horrified that I was a human being, horrified that I had to sit there on that cliff having nowhere to go. I even contemplated asking for rescue but soon realized how I feared helicopters, that I would not even be able to board one on the steep edge.

There I sat, believing once again that I was stuck, alone and afraid. There was no way out! I continued to cry and was inconsolable. I hated that I was alive. I hated being so vulnerable, so helpless, so out of control. I had no idea what I would do. For about fifteen or 20 minutes of panic, I realized there was only one thing I could think to do. I would ask God for help. I decided to do this, despite doubtful thoughts. I cried out in my mind, "God, I have no idea how you can help me, I see no way out, please help me Lord." What seemed like only moments later, a man who noticed I was hysterical came over to us. He asked Keena and Carl what was wrong. He then approached me, sharing that he had actually run over this path countless times. Finally, I looked up and noticed this man had a surety in his spirit that spoke to me. It was a strong, calm presence that was completely stable and immediately comforting. He exuded confidence in his own personal safety, stating, "I'm going to take you by the hand and walk you across that bridge." He extended his arm saying, "Take my hand and I will lead you. Do not look down, just look straight ahead." I took his hand and we walked straight across those steps in the sky. It was amazing. Not only did I reach the top; I got to feel something completely new. I experienced a certainty in my own personal safety. This gift for my soul was provided because I had asked God for help. Hardly a moment had gone by before God granted my request. He saw to my need in a way I could not have foreseen. I was literally handed victory over fear, feelings of calm and peace in high places.

Bottom line, when we ask, it is given! In the same way I was aided, you will be also. Never forget when you are afraid, feeling hopeless, and cannot see through the darkness, that God will always help when you cry out to Him. He never abandons you, immediately coming to your aide. Whether seen or unseen, He is at work in your life, in your moment of need. Have faith, ask, and be ready to receive His help.

I feel I had this experience only months before I was diagnosed so that I could be prepared, shown how to deal with my upcoming trial.

⌘

POSSIBLE TERMINAL ILLNESS

AS WE KNOW, LIFE IS NOT permanent. If you have been told you are terminally ill it means you are headed to the same place as everyone else. Even so, being slapped in the face with your own mortality can cause terror that may lead one to make irrational choices. This instant collision with the reality of cancer (no matter the stage or type) is still not a reason to fly off the handle and start recklessly spending your life energy. Take care and prevent yourself from racing toward anything that will destroy the remaining health that you have. It is true that this energy/health is being challenged at this point in time. It makes sense to find out why it is challenged, and see where the cause lies. Basic testing is wise. A viral panel can reveal the presence of any viruses that may be burdening your immune system and distracting it from killing cancer.

Refer to the reference section of this book for a brief list of labs that will perform these tests. To gather information now about your health and be an investigator, will help in making decisions about your own treatment and healing journey. Yes, it is urgent when one receives a cancer diagnosis. However, it is not the best course of action to rush into things because one is fearful. Rushing is never a good idea, as it leaves no time for contemplation, research, or meditation. This is not to say wait around for months while you mull things over. It is merely a reminder that you have time to collect the necessary data to make informed choices and proceed with caution on a healing path that is both effective and beneficial to you in every way possible.

⌘

LET THE HEALING BEGIN

LET THE HEALING BEGIN! The first place I went was an acupuncturist. When I was leaving this doctor's office on the first day of treatment, I happened to see an old woman struggling on a curb, her husband ordering her to get to the sidewalk. Her feet were far apart with one hand balancing her on a parking meter: she was obviously in peril. I hurried over to assist, and as I did, I shared with her that I was headed to USC Norris Center for surgery. She then shared some of her own story: she had been a patient at USC Norris Center years ago and they had made her well. "That's my place," she said. "My husband got well there too!" I felt encouraged by this.

Yet another encouragement was an analogy the acupuncturist made to me in the office. I decided to think on this instead of dreading anything dark in my future. He said something to this effect: "Have you ever seen Indiana Jones where Harrison Ford is standing very still while being attacked by a man who happens to be a pro with a whip? Well, after a large display of more than competent whirling around and slicing parts of Harrison's clothes off, the enemy looks to Harrison who is standing completely still. Then, Harrison lifts his gun and simply shoots him dead." The evil man with the whip is the cancer while God, the doctors and I are the gun. I can be still and peaceful while the cancer whirls around my life showing a display of false power. Then, zap – it will be gone.

⌘

VISUALIZATION

1. LET THE LIGHT BATHE YOUR CELLS.
2. Let yourself become enveloped by the light.
3. Picture the sick part of yourself leaving the room, let go of it.

Once, while I was at the acupuncturist, I saw many dark spots. Then, I saw little points of light poking through each one until each spot was washed over with light. I realized I was seeing cancer cells in my mind's eye.

After each dark cell was bathed in the light I saw a light that totally enveloped everything. Soon after this occurred, I had what I would call a vision: I saw the sick part of myself getting up off of the table and leaving the room. The sick part of me literally had walked out the door. This was an incredible time of healing.

On that day as I left the office with my aunt Rachelle I felt the energy of light in the core of my being. I told Rachelle that I felt a certainty I would live through this trial. This time of healing seemed miraculous and I thanked God for it. Of course, this was very early on, even before surgery. I share this experience as visualizations you may wish to keep in mind while participating in your own healing.

⌘

TRUST YOURSELF

IN ORDER TO BECOME HEALTHY as a society, we not only need to avoid illness but we should seek health in all that we do. We need to help our bodies and minds to be strong and eliminate anything in our lives that contributes to disease.

I would encourage you, who recently may have been diagnosed with cancer, and are under the stress of dealing with this disease, to *trust* yourself. Make a deep commitment to take responsibility for your own health. Pay close attention to how you feel about the situation, information you have been given, etcetera. For example, consider the people you choose to be around, the foods you eat, and the environment in which you spend your time. It is critical while making important decisions that you remain fearless. Recognize fear as an indicator that you are possibly in the wrong place or contemplating a wrong choice. Your decisions must come from full faith, hope, surety, and trust. When you are hopeful, it is an indication you are in the right place and moving forward in the right direction.

Do not be in a rush. I cannot stress this enough. Please do not run, but walk toward your decisions carefully and methodically, giving yourself time to view the entire picture of your healing. If you rush, you may be missing important information you need to consider as you plan to move forward. For example, if your doctor says you will die if you don't follow his/her advice immediately, step back and take a deep breath. Fully realize that you are responsible for your health, regardless of whether anyone likes your decisions or not. Realize that you have the time to make a decision that you should be sure about, regardless of the outcome. The only way this can happen is if you use acquired knowledge, good common sense, intuition, and divine guidance. Think about your body and what it needs to function properly. Remember your immune system is still working and it needs more attention from you in order to function better. Trust that your immune system has gotten you through so far, and it continues fighting even now. Use the tools in the workbook to find out why your immune system is not performing to its full capacity. The tools will help guide you to the best choices you can make in order to bolster and protect your immune system as you choose treatment options to rid your body of cancer.

Ultimately it is your immune system that will recognize and kill the cancer. Medical treatment and medicine you take can kill cancer and bring down the personal load of cancer cells you are carrying in your body. However, your ultimate weapon is your immune system, so protect it, become mindful and aware that you need it to serve as the major player against your specific cancer. As much as medicine can slow the process, you want to make sure that any dormant metastatic cells that are left in your body after treatment are taken out by your immune system. This will give you an advantage and leave you at little to no risk for recurrence. Realize this truth: when your immune system recognizes the cancer as a foreign cell, it can easily and readily fight it, clearing your body of all abnormal cells when we give it the physical and mental support it needs.

⌘

WHEN AN ANGEL VISITS

I HAVE AN EXTRAORDINARY FRIEND named Sherry. She continually amazes me with her love and compassion. I even wrote her mother a letter once to convey the respect and admiration I had and still have for her awesome ability to be a loving companion and a true friend whom I could rely on always with trust and openness. I even dreamt of Sherry once; that she used to live among the stars and teach others how to love one another. I think that sums up how loving she is. What an amazing being!

She is also one to hold strong beliefs in what others may doubt. I could always share my wild spiritual experiences and dreams with her. They were never met with shock or awe, just a great dialogue about the experience.

When I began my healing journey she immediately said, "I'm going to ask Archangel Gabriel to help you." Of course I appreciated this, but never expected anything to come of it. Imagine my surprise when a few days later I was receiving acupuncture and something astonishing occurred. I was meditating and relaxing on the table as usual when all of the sudden I saw a figure standing next to me. There was a large torso and arm, with very large muscles. I looked up and realized that I was not looking at a mere mortal but an Angel. I understood that the imagery of Archangel Gabriel had come to visit me just as Sherry had requested. I was truly amazed. We are never alone.

⌘

COLD AND FLU MINDSET

WHENEVER I HAD A HEALTH ISSUE during my life, I usually approached it the same way every time. I would look to where the weakness was and then find ways to heal my body. Sometimes, it was more urgent, and required the use of conventional medicine for symptom control. Then, I would begin treating the cause by more natural means. Each ailment had its own requirements but I was always mindful to get to the "root of the problem" to remain free from chronic issues or weaknesses. When diagnosed with cancer, after the initial shock, I began thinking about it in a similar fashion.

I believe that when it comes to cancer treatment, we should consider the disease in a similar way to a cold or flu. When we have a cold or flu what do we normally do? We take good care of ourselves. We look to food as a source of wellness. We stay in comfortable temperatures and we avoid anything that may further burden our immune systems. We instinctively shelter ourselves and know that we're going to have to nurture the body and then wait it out. We have an expectation that overcoming the flu may be a process with a marked beginning, middle and end. We don't rush the process because we have a general idea of the time frame. This process may take a week or it may take three weeks.

Even though people do die from the flu, we do not panic. We have confidence it will resolve itself and importantly, we always give ourselves *time* to get well, and we don't feel bad for isolating ourselves or doing extra things to nurture our bodies and minds. We rest more and listen to our bodies for what they want at each moment. My opinion is that we should treat cancer with this kind of patience. A good diet, lots of rest, lack of fearfulness, trusting in the process, and giving the body time and room to heal effectively. This may be a long process spanning six months to six years. You need to do all you can to heal the cancer but taking your time will allow you to have the patience to be kind to yourself, and to remain self-protective.

⌘

THE CROSS AND THE LIGHT

I'VE HAD TWO CROSS NECKLACES in my life, each of which were gifts to me. I always liked the idea of receiving a cross from another person as opposed to buying one for myself. Something about it just feels right and in line with the entire concept of what the cross represents: a gift offered, then accepted.

Sometime after my hysterectomy, my mother sent me a cross that she owned, which was a gift from her husband. I was so happy to receive this cross and put it on right away. The very first night I wore it I had the following dream: a person who I thought to be my mother dressed all in white was moving around high above me, in a tree. She sprinkled what looked like raindrops from her hands. The drops showered down upon me, but as the shower fell, instead of feeling rain, I realized it was a shower of light.

In the days that followed I saw that light almost daily. My interpretation was that I was touched by the light of the world, the perfect and intelligent light that heals everything and resides in all of us: the light that comes from a gift received. I meditated on this light often and considered it to be contained within my cells, healing me daily. This gave me comfort. Later, I dreamt of the light once again. This time I saw each particle of light and inside one particle I found all intelligence, all perfection. Every particle was the same and held the power of having entire, complete, and cohesive strength on its own.

In my mind, I associated this gift of light with the cross I had received. I felt it was a timely reminder of what is available to me as a believer in Christ, and that God's perfect light is always with me, working in perfect grace to bring healing and truth into my body and my life. A reminder that God sent his son, who claimed to be the light of the world and indeed that light resides in me and in all of us.

⌘

NOTHING NATURAL

I WAS RAISED IN A FAMILY THAT took a lot of responsibility for their health. An active nurturing of the body when ill was the modus operandi. Therefore, I was interested in natural medicine and educating myself on how to aid the body in its own healing processes. I read many books on health and healing growing up and particularly liked books by Edgar Cayce. Since I have personally experienced the great effectiveness of using natural resources for health and healing, I believe it's important to understand that nothing natural will be offered to you if you seek healing advice only from conventional medicine. You're not likely to receive counsel on even the most basic information on how to take care of your health, like nutrition.

In the last few decades, natural resources have often been "unproven" to treat serious illnesses like cancer, primarily because they are not patented, therefore unprofitable. There is little to no incentive for those who are truly interested in testing these natural resources for effectiveness against illness. Because they are not widely used, and the FDA has not approved them, you may be discouraged from seeking natural treatments. It is important to realize that a conventional doctor is a member of the American Medical Association (and therefore regulated by the FDA) and therefore s/he will also either deny the usefulness of such products and resources or worse, have little to no knowledge about them. I touch on this lightly to point out one limitation you will experience when treated within the western model of medicine, and to encourage awareness of how these limitations might impact you as a patient. I also mention it to encourage both finding and receiving the most effective cancer treatment available for your specific cancer type.

⌘

FAULTY EVIDENCE

I WAS STAGE 1A AFTER SURGERY. At that time my doctor mentioned an optional one-time radiation treatment as prevention for recurrence. She said it was completely up to me and the treatment was not necessary but "optional." My immediate thought was that I would not choose radiation if I had the option to say no. I had researched radiation in the past and had zero confidence in the treatment. When I returned for a follow-up appointment my doctor had significantly changed her attitude about the radiation treatment. She pressed me to undergo the treatment and was insistent that I needed it. She proposed that I go to a consultation with a radiologist to "at least listen." I was pretty resistant but after several pleadings from my doctor, I ended up going to a consultation.

Accompanied by my husband and aunt, I asked the radiologist many questions. What was the rate of success? What was the difference between the rate of recurrence with and without the radiation? I also found out the specifics of what was going to be done. The radiation treatment called high-dose rate (HDR) brachytherapy, consisted of radioactive pellets emitting dosages of radiation from a catheter placed inside the vaginal canal. The recommendation was three sessions of this treatment. When I asked the radiologist about side-effects, she casually rattled off the possibilities: burning of the bladder, similar to a chronic bladder infection for an indefinite length of time, a scaring or blockage could form in my lower intestines, which may have to be surgically removed, and irritable bowel syndrome, as I would certainly receive a high dose of radiation to my colon, bladder, and gut. When I asked how to protect the colon, bladder, and intestines, I was informed exposure could not be avoided. My vaginal canal would also likely be burned and scarred with a high risk of shrinkage and a possibility that the vaginal canal could close completely. I was offered "vaginal stretchers" to insert during and after the treatments to prevent closure. It was disconcerting that each time I asked the radiologist about success rates or other details, she had no answer except to say, "all the information is in this study," gesturing to the papers she held in her hand.

At home I reviewed the study, which had no answers to my specific questions. This particular study merely explained the difference between types of delivery for the radiation, i.e. high dose versus low dose, and frequency. Reflecting back, the only thing I was sure of after the consultation was that I was going to suffer terrible side effects and I had no clue about how it could really benefit me. The thought of making such an important decision based on inadequate evidence was completely unacceptable, so I decided to begin my own research. After reading through hundreds of studies on PubMed, I came to my conclusion, which was this: if I used radiation as a preventative for recurrence and then in fact had a recurrence, I could not use it again. More importantly, if I underwent radiation before I had a recurrence, I was much less likely to be cured by radiation when it mattered. Finally, there was a high probability I would not be able to receive any further surgery after brachytherapy, because of the damage to the tissue, which compromises the ability to heal. Why waste the one bullet in my arsenal? The radiation would be more likely to be the most effective and curative for a recurrence of cancer, as opposed to preventing it.

To me, brachytherapy sounds like a spa treatment. However, just because something is given a name that sounds non-threatening and is presented as "private," "targeted," "outpatient," or "brief," does not mean it is in any way safe, protective, efficient, or necessary.

After my recurrence, brachytherapy was recommended again. I could not comprehend this. How could I possibly allow myself to succumb to what I believed to be a barbaric practice with major consequences to my quality of life?

Although I was told the recommended radiation treatments were necessary if I wanted to live, I could not find evidence of this fact. When researching mortality rates of those who had the treatments and those who did not, the percentage differences were nominal. I could not justify allowing this treatment with such faulty evidence of a real effect on the cancer.

At this point, I traveled back to Arizona where I received treatment proposals from two different centers. I wanted to find a way around this brachytherapy.

⌘

YOU WANT ME TO DO WHAT?

HAVING A SPECIFIC TYPE OF cancer qualifies you to be mainstreamed into the standard of care for that cancer. You are given the same chosen treatment protocols everyone else receives with that specific cancer. For example, all women with uterine cancer are treated with the chemotherapy drug Cisplatin.

In my case, however, my physician at Envita Medical Center, had ordered a tumor profile provided by Caris Life Sciences. This is not what usually occurs within the standard of care. Normally this test, which is considered experimental, is utilized only if standardized treatments have failed; it becomes part of a last ditch effort to save your life. In my case, the tumor profile gave the doctor important, personalized information about my specific tumor, providing a list of agents with potential clinical benefit alongside a list of ineffective treatments. To my surprise, Cisplatin was on the ineffective side, making it a bad choice to treat my cancer with it.

Two treatment plans were proposed when I had stage IIIB, metastatic and aggressive uterine cancer. One plan was by Cancer Treatment Centers of America (plan A), while the other was by Envita

Medical Center (plan B). Plan A included eight rounds of chemotherapy with Cisplatin, followed by approximately 38 radiation treatments, both internal brachytherapy, and external beam full pelvic area. After conclusion of the chemo, brachytherapy, and external full pelvic radiation, I would receive an additional eight rounds of chemotherapy.

As icing on the cake, I was to return for chemotherapy treatments with Cisplatin once a year, for the rest of my life in order to prevent recurrence. Upon hearing this I asked the doctor how the results of my tumor profile affected his decision about the proposed treatment. He replied, "I don't care about that, the test is considered experimental and is only used in rare cases. We consider that information only after other treatments have failed." This doctor was adamant that I would be taking a large risk if I chose to operate outside the customary protocol for uterine cancer patients. He exuded confidence that he would save my life by following this standard protocol.

Only after Cisplatin fails, would he consider additional scientific information regarding my specific situation. Was I incorrect in concluding that my specific type of cancer fell into the rare category that he had first identified?

Freedom from fear enabled me to think clearly enough to consider my options. I considered plan B. It included a mixture of drugs listed as effective for my specific tumor: a cocktail of three chemotherapy drugs, plus a fourth natural chemo drug also on the list. I questioned another doctor about plan A. He said, "Well, first of all, if you use a drug that is not listed as effective on the Caris report, you are already starting off at 50% less effective. To rely on just one chemo drug is a very bad idea, too large of a risk." You don't want to ruin your one good chance at winning your fight to live by choosing a drug that will only waste your immune system, weaken you, and leave you with your body's inability to get rid of the cancer.

You don't want to be given the wrong treatment or chemotherapy drug. To be sure your doctor is recommending a treatment you can rely on, it would be wise to order tumor profiling from Caris Life Sciences. By reviewing biomarkers and using molecular profiling, the test yields a list of effective chemotherapy drugs and other possible effective agents that would be favorable treatments for your cancer. Be sure to request that the hospital keep samples of your tumor for five years after surgery. It may be wise to get the test done right away, regardless of what stage the cancer is diagnosed to be. This way, you have the information to move forward if you end up with metastatic cancer or a recurrence in the future. You can request this test and read about it at CarisLifeSciences.com.

Even though this test has been in existence for over twenty years, most doctors will tell you it is only used in rare cases, and will not order the test, because it is outside the standard of care protocol. Do not wait to use this test until other treatments fail. Give yourself the best chance at survival by making sure your body is not weakened by the wrong treatments initially. Remember, what you choose in the beginning can be the most effective, because your immune system will be strongest at the start.

Obviously, you want to make good initial choices to capitalize on your first chance to utilize the appropriate treatment choice in terms of chemotherapy drugs. Take the time to collect this critical information about your specific cancer and what will work to kill it. In my case, results arrived within five days, but even if it takes two weeks, remain calm. Arm yourself with this imperative information before you agree to, or make any decision regarding your proposed treatment options.

Unfortunately, you may have to pay for this test out of pocket. It will be money well spent.

⌘

A BEAUTIFUL QUILT

MY FRIEND LAURA MAKES QUILTS for people who have cancer. She started one for me after I was first diagnosed with stage 1A cancer. She told me several times she agonized over the fact that it had taken her so long to get it completed. However, she happened to finish it soon after I was diagnosed again with metastatic uterine cancer. At that time she brought the quilt to my house. Standing in the living room, she spread it out in front of me. Suddenly, all of my fondest, joyful, childhood memories came to light. A beautiful sensation washed over me as I found many lost, forgotten moments. This experience flooded me with assurance that I had been loved. I remembered this important truth with a smile. This blanket accompanied me during my darkest moments. I remain inspired by its visual beauty, made with love and scripture sewn across its borders. Thank you, Laura for your artistic talents and caring in a time of great need.

⌘

IMAGE OF MARY

WHILE UNDERGOING CHEMOTHERAPY I was often in bed. Extremely weak and fatigued, I had no energy to move. I worked hard to think positively, and I meditated regularly. The result was a heightened spiritual consciousness. One day, while meditating, I thought of Mother Mary and I said her prayer aloud,

Hail Mary, full of grace, the Lord is with thee.
Blessed art thou among women,
And blessed is the fruit of thy womb, Jesus.
Holy Mary, Mother of God, pray for us sinners
Now and at the hour of our death.
Amen.

Shortly after, Mary appeared in a dream.

March 12, 2012

I had a dream last night. First, I encountered my doctor, who briefly examined me. She discovered cancer on my chest and then biopsied it. Then I went off with some friends to a place similar to a baseball field near batting cages. It was there I saw people lying down on their stomachs, side by side on the ground. Once I realized they were praying to Mother Mary, I looked around for her. I saw Mary standing amongst other women all of whom were wearing bonnets. Mary was dressed in black. She looked like a normal woman, somewhat plain.

I decided to approach her and ask her, "Please heal me?" Mary replied only with action. As she extended her hands toward me, I watched as light particles passed through them. This light traveled my way and enveloped my entire body. In the dream, Mary had given me the imagery of the light of God, which healed me. In the dream I was aware the healing from cancer had been complete.

⌘

RICHARD

RICHARD IS A GOOD EXAMPLE OF a person who fully participated in his own healing. He indeed set the stage for his miracle. Here is his story.

After he contracted Valley fever he was very ill. The doctor had showed him his lungs on an x-ray. He recommended that one of the lungs be removed because there was a hole the size of a fifty-cent piece. His lung had additional damage from spores, which were embedded there. Richard refused to allow the doctor to schedule the surgery for the lung removal. He wanted to believe his lung could and would heal.

After months of struggling with bronchitis, pneumonia, and a fever, he decided to go on a prayer retreat. He was prayed over, encouraged, and given hope. Instead of resting, even though he felt feverish, sweaty, had chills and difficulty breathing, he woke up early in the morning and took off running.

He felt he had a leading from the Lord to run as fast as he could. He didn't question this. Despite feeling terrible he pushed on. He did this everyday while on the retreat and after two weeks or so he went back to the doctor for a scan.

The doctor was amazed that the scan showed no hole in the lung. He didn't think it possible and said, "This can't be the same pair of lungs!"

Today Richard is whole and healed. When in peril, he had a group of people who decided he was whole, healed, and strong. He also refused to believe a lie presented as the truth about his lung being unable to heal. The lie that told him his best hope was a very limited quality of life.

He was a full participant in his own healing. He relied on faith, he was obedient to divine guidance, and he did not accept anything short of full healing. He did not allow damage to the body. He set the stage for his miracle and then he experienced the miracle of his healing.

⌘

FEAR OVERCOME

WHEN I WAS DIAGNOSED WITH cancer, I immediately associated the word with death. In order to prevent fear from clouding my judgment in the midst of having to make critical decisions about my health and treatment plan, I had to confront my fear of dying. Others feared for my life as well, but I had to sit quietly and deal with my own mortality.

The fear of death is best kept in perspective. Hope empowers us from the start, allowing for clarity of thought during the task of decision-making. Acknowledging death, facing it, is one way to avoid being controlled by it. None of us know what the outcome of our diagnosis will be. What we do know is that cancer cannot "kill us" or "take us" anywhere, because we have been given the gift of eternal life. Our hope and faith in God can defeat fear, which rears its ugly head when we feel anxious, alone, or isolated.

To remain empowered and clear, I chose to recognize that the idea that "cancer holds the power of death" over us is a false notion. Whether I was talking with a friend who was scared of the choices I was making, or looking to a professional for guidance, not only did I have to overcome my own fear, but theirs as well. Accomplishing this was difficult. Remaining hopeful and knowing that God is in control, knowing that He is the glorious physician, the healer and the King, brought me peace.

Peace I leave with you; my peace I give to you. I do not give to you as the world gives. Do not let your hearts be troubled and do not be afraid.

—John 14:27 (NIV)

Accepting an empowered state of being is essential in defeating the illusions of helplessness, becoming overwhelmed, or paralyzed with inaction.

Most importantly, fear attempts to deceive us into giving up our authority. Our power and authority are "one," and should not, under any circumstance, be diminished or compromised. When fear emerges, it is easy to set aside good judgment, because there is usually a thick blanket of negativity and fear associated with our thoughts of death.

In my experience, there is an expectation that one should listen to and believe all that is said in the professional world regarding the facts about cancer. I was expected to stay on the course of action that was planned for me by others. This type of cooperation may have sometimes arisen from a fear of cancer and death. This was the case regarding recommended radiation treatments. Quite a few radiologists insisted over 48 radiation treatments were necessary to eradicate cancer. One went as far as to say that studies over the years had proven this to be true. However, I believed that all circumstances are unique, and when remission came after four radiation sessions, I did not place my faith in the claims of the radiologists or proven studies. I relied on the claim of the true healer, God. Instead of giving control of my health to the radiologist, I embraced hope and believed that it was possible I had completed my radiation after four treatments. Indeed there is no limit to how or when you may be healed from affliction.

Praise the Lord, O my soul, and forget not all his benefits, who forgives all your sins and heals all your diseases, who redeems your life from the pit and crowns you with love and compassion.

—Psalm 103:2-4 (NIV)

He said to her, "Daughter, your faith has healed you. Go in peace and be freed from your suffering."

—Mark 5:34 (NIV)

I can only imagine that I would have been more damaged by unnecessary radiation treatments than by refusing them. I could have easily remained in a fearful place by believing that if I went against the "proven" studies and the insistence of the "expert radiologist" I would be putting my life at risk. It was my personal understanding that there is no safe level of ionized radiation for human tissue. Radiation is one of the major causes of cancer, and I couldn't imagine that it would heal mine.

So, do not be deceived into handing over your authority to anyone you believe can alleviate your fear, stress, or anxiety concerning death. Specifically, this means any person or professional who claims they can "save you" from death.

Considering death at this point in your life is productive. Give your vulnerable self, the one that has to experience death one day, over to the divine. Ask God for His protection. If you are able, make peace with death. Realize that no matter when you experience death, God will be right there with you, at your side as your protector.

When I was in darkness and fear, this prayer helped me to become centered, peaceful.

"Dear Lord, take my hand now. Hold me near as you guide me personally through whatever your assignment is for me. Never let go and never be away from me. As we walk through this together, I will fear no evil. I know you are with me. You are my protection and the destroyer of death. I trust in you Father, to guide me directly into health, removing from me anything that is rooted in evil. I have asked and I know it has been given. You have promised me all good things. I receive your promises and praise you now for my perfect health, and for conquering death, the last enemy. In Jesus name I pray, Amen."

Knowing that healing is at work in your life, the physical body will begin to catch up to the spiritual body, the one that is perfect and healthy, and the body you inherited through Christ's sacrifice.

"For I know the plans I have for you," says the Lord. "Plans for good and not for harm, plans to give you a future and a hope."

—Jeremiah 29:11

Now you are free to listen for guidance from the divine. Hold to the truth; know that you will be guided by your hope and faith. You will be freed from fear. The reality of imminent threat is eliminated. As treatment plans are presented to you (by those who believe in them), be encouraged that you are able to recognize any untruth. Georges Braque (1964) says, "Truth exists. Only lies are invented." Remain quiet and steadfast, stay hopeful, and believe only those things that resonate as positive, full of promise, and true. Do not allow the voice of fear and deception to dictate any of your choices on your path to victory over cancer:

I tore myself away from the safe comfort of certainties through my love for truth; and truth rewarded me.

—Sylvia Ashton-Warner

Nothing is as powerful as the real truth—your truth—the truth of who you are. Your ability to overcome, to heal, and to honor yourself throughout the healing process, with divine guidance at your side, remains fully intact.

Faith will break the power of him who holds the power of death – that is, the 'foe of God' (fear) and free those who all their lives were held in slavery by their fear of death.

—Hebrews 2:15

⌘

SET THE STAGE

WHEN I WAS VERY ILL, A professional healer who specialized in deliverance was recommended to me. I was unfamiliar with the practice but thought it may be a good idea to see what he offered. When I met the man who had a ministry of deliverance, he gave me an explanation of deliverance and why it needed to be done. He explained that deliverance was a revived ministry that holds some illness is born out of "spiritual warfare." It had never occurred to me that a spiritual enemy might wish to oppress me or undermine my strength, injure me, and keep me from my potential of having a productive healthy life.

I told him immediately that I trusted God but questioned what His will for me was. He was certain of his answer, that God wanted me healed and he cited scriptures to prove it. Further, that God wanted me to be strong and well so that I could glorify Him. He said there was no question in this.

I was astounded. I was relieved that I didn't have to guess at what God wanted for me. I knew He wanted me whole. The session lasted at least an hour. During this time and to my surprise I experienced warmth in my abdominal area. This indicated that healing was indeed occurring. Before the session even began, "signs or symptoms of negativity leaving the body" were described to me, and I experienced some of these symptoms. Admittedly, it was an unusual situation and despite my skepticisms I felt it was extremely beneficial.

After the session I felt I should continue the practice of deliverance. I began to say a simple prayer, "In the name of Jesus, I command anything rooted in darkness to leave my body at once." Along with this prayer, I praised God for all of His blessings and also what I did not like, i.e. the cancer. I praised Him in spite of everything, for my suffering, for my cancer and for giving his only son so that I could have life, and have it abundantly.

Because it felt so powerful to praise Him, I began speaking to Him in my mind and aloud almost continuously for a period of time. It was as if I could feel a power building up inside of my body. I thanked God for sending the Holy Spirit after Jesus departed from us. Praising Him was a powerful healing asset.

This was a major force in setting the stage for receiving my miracle. I fully participated in my own healing. I was called to different spiritual practices along my healing journey. They were shifting and changing practices but when I felt lead by the Spirit, I would act.

There were times when I felt like I was going backwards in my attempt at healing. I had fears that I was trapped by the illness. These were the times I had to choose hope over fear, again and again.

My two-year struggle seemed long and at times I had been devastated, believing the plan had failed. Facts of my growing tumor came to light, which caused doubt. Doubt in my choices, doubt in my tactics, doubt in my belief. I questioned whether or not I had been wrong to listen for divine guidance. After all, those choices, that guidance, had led me to a point that looked a lot like failure. The real difficulty was facing my doctor who informed I was at a critical point and was going to die if I didn't undergo conventional therapies immediately. There were times where I almost sunk into the temptation of fear, sinking into a black hole of despair, unbelief. Facing one view of the "facts" (my cancer had grown rapidly, I was in peril, in a rush), I broadened my mind, I leapt toward hope, and I looked in the mirror. Despite the illness, I looked and felt stronger than I had in years. I acknowledged that I had no good thing apart from God. I was vulnerable, and completely reliant on His grace. I praised God for His personal care that He has for all of us. I praised Him for his protection during every hour of every day of my life. I praised Him for taking care of me then, now and always. He became my first love.

A cancer patient shared her doubt about a beautiful experience she had. She had a choice to make. She could believe the message that was conveyed to her spirit or she could believe in the current physical state she was in, that she was stuck in illness.

Upon waking around 4 AM one morning, she was reminded of my healing. She was suddenly informed by grace that what happened for me was happening to her. She wondered if she could really be like me. She questioned me about this and had a lot of doubt about the entire experience. She said things like, "Could that really happen to me? Or was that just a rare thing that only happened to you?" Her thinking implied I could be somehow different from her, special. I was thrilled with the opportunity to assure her, to tell her what had been conveyed to me years ago: She was the daughter of a King. She inherited God's promises through the blood of Jesus and thus she had rights, authority, and the promise of health.

She said, "I've had hands laid on me before and I'm still battling this disease." She complained it had been four years and she felt time had been wasted on bad choices and the wrong treatments, while her cancer worsened. I shared certain elements of my healing, specifically those involving disappointment and doubt.

With this I was able to encourage her trust in the timing of her decisions, and I was happy to share my personal belief that healing begins on the spiritual or energetic plane and over time manifests in the physical body. I shared with her how early on a woman prayed with me, for me, faithfully claiming there was not spot in me, no imperfection because I had been perfected by Jesus' sacrifice.

Setting the stage for a miracle required certain thoughts and actions on my part, and below is a partial list of those requirements.

1. Accepting and believing without any doubt that I was already whole, already healed.
2. Claiming my healing as true, before it was revealed in the physical body.
3. Holding a somewhat dismissive attitude or minimal focus on anything unhealthy revealed in the flesh. For example, an MRI, which shows a tumor today was not so discouraging when I recognized the MRI as being merely a snapshot in time. That moment had already passed and that picture could change at any moment.
4. Placing my complete trust and faith in Him.
5. Staying my mind on that which is good. Philippians 4:8,

"Finally, brothers, whatever is true, whatever is honorable, whatever is just, whatever is pure, whatever is lovely, whatever is commendable, if there is any excellence, if there is anything worthy of praise, think about these things."

6. Praising Him for everything. Psalm 7:17 (ESV), "I will give to the Lord the thanks due to his righteousness, and I will sing praise to the name of the Lord, the Most High."

7. Reciting, "I in He, He in me." Believing His Divine intelligence, His perfection resides within me.

8. Deliverance – Asking to be freed from illness. Psalm 91:15, Believing as I call upon Him, He will answer me: He will be with me when I am in trouble, He will deliver me. Stating a simple command, "In the name of Jesus I command all roots of illness, infirmity and anything rooted in darkness to come out of me." You can specify your ailment(s), for example, "I command all roots of uterine cancer to come out of me in the name of Jesus, Amen."

9. Having faith that once it is asked in His name, it is given. Matthew 7:7 (NIV), "Ask and it will be given to you; seek and you will find; knock and the door will be opened to you."

⌘

ONE BEAUTIFUL WOMAN

IT'S THE YEAR 2003. I'M IN MY CAR driving to Santa Monica. I'm driving on Wilshire, looking at people in cars next to me, and somehow they all seem familiar. What is confusing me is that each person I see I vaguely recognize as a distant relative or friend, and yet, I cannot identify these people either by name or appearance.

As I await the red light to glow green, a woman appears, crossing the street in front of my car. Although this woman seemed ordinary, my experience of her was far outside the normal realm. As I glimpsed her, I gasped as the true beauty of my fellow human literally knocked the wind out of me. In this moment, with my consciousness raised, I sat breathless, in awe of her beauty. After I caught my breath and drove off, I contemplated this phenomenon. It was my thinking that "recognition" of others was a type of being connected to a truth, that people are indeed related to me. Those people were "familiar" as if they were my brothers and my sisters, family. The bible says that we are sisters and brothers in the Lord. Reading these words was completely different from experiencing the magnitude of this truth.

When my senses are dulled, oftentimes I remember this and it brings joy and remembrance that we can all help one another because we are so very close.

Though a fleeting experience, it remains a powerful reminder to love others and myself, and that we are all magnificently beautiful. I imagine that if we really could always see clearly, we might always experience the beauty of others, and that it would take our breath away. These beautiful people, our kin: we are all one family.

⌘

DO NO HARM

LIKE MOST AMERICANS, AFTER MY cancer diagnosis, I was offered surgery, chemotherapy, and radiation. It is worth noting that it took well over seventeen treatment options to rid my body of an aggressive stage IIIB metastatic uterine cancer. This was far beyond the standard, and grossly limiting, three choices offered in traditional medicine. I believe my ability to draw from a greater number of choices led me to my healing. Keeping in mind a broader perspective and eliminating limitation allowed me to attack my cancer with more strength. Embracing more than the standard options offered by the western medical model might save your life.

As I've said before, I was no stranger to natural medicine used in combination or as an adjunct therapy to traditional medicine. Having cancer presented the same problems as having any other ailment, in the sense that my options were very limited if I remained within the traditional model. This leads me to address the issue of the limitations your doctor may have as a licensed member of the American Medical Association (AMA). It was important that I kept even my doctor's limitations in mind while looking for answers on my healing path.

Doctors take the Hippocratic oath in medical school, which in the past acted as a binding contract for physicians. The first and critical point in the oath is, "Do no harm." Today's version may say, "I will apply, for the benefit of the sick, all measures [that] are required, avoiding those twin traps of overtreatment and therapeutic nihilism" (Tyson, PBS.org). Since all doctors swear this oath to do no harm, one may ask several questions. What has chipped away at a doctor's ability to keep this oath in caring for you and doing all s/he can to avoid harm to you in the process? Why is your doctor limited by law to offer few options after cancer diagnosis?

Another concept I thought about constantly was the idea of giving all authority to my doctor. As we are conditioned to place our immediate and complete trust in doctors, the natural response results in a submissive type of relationship to them, rarely questioning their authority and expertise. However, your allopathic (traditional) doctor, who is licensed by the AMA, must work within a system that is fundamentally flawed, controlled, and tainted by pharmaceutical companies. There is little doubt conventionally trained doctors have been influenced by pharmaceutical corporations. This influence puts us at risk and in an unfortunate position. When it comes to medicine, as with all other purchases, the buyer should beware. Additionally, it is important to question a doctor's recommendations and demand enough scientific evidence to show that your treatment option is the most effective for your ailment.

Many conventional doctors have their hands tied as they try to do their good work. I write this not to attack these well-meaning people, but only to point out how this limited system affects your choices. Take heed and investigate what paradigm each doctor you hire is working within so that you can utilize the available tools to steer your own course of treatment choices.

The problem is, in a nutshell, as Bob Beck once quipped, "A patient cured is a customer lost" (cancertutor.com). The cancer industry, the AMA, and pharmaceutical companies don't want cures. They want expensive treatments.

This problem has arisen over many decades. To summarize, in the 1800's, there were homeopathic and allopathic doctors. Allopathic, or conventional, medicine offered treatments such as bloodletting, surgery, and dosing patients with lead, mercury, and other toxins, all of which were dangerous and could kill the body. This was opposed to the homeopathic model, which offered to stimulate the body's natural healing process with natural, non-toxic means, causing the death of the disease, and allowing the body to live and thrive. This method was based on old European/Indian teachings stemming from observation and experience of proven results. As allopathic medicine was less effective and in fact, dangerous, it had to be both defended and presented as a valid choice in medicine. This defensive action was intentional, well thought out, and aggressive. A type of silent warfare was waged to undermine and eradicate homeopathic doctors who presented competition to the new model.

After the turn of the century, the AMA joined with the financial sector to transform allopathic medicine into a new force: the medical economy.

In this new economy, doctors were taught to prescribe pharmaceutical drugs, perform surgical procedures, and do expensive diagnostic testing. Educational standards and licensing regulations were changed to exclude natural medicine and soon only members of the AMA could practice medicine legally. To this day, doctors receive instruction for drug-centered medicine and also are educated further through Continuing Medical Education courses, which are largely funded by the pharmaceutical industry (Drugwatch.com, 2015). All of this has resulted in legislation, making it illegal for any doctor to give recommendations for cancer treatments other than radiation, surgery, and chemotherapy, all of which are extremely expensive. I recommend a documentary, "Under Our Skin" and video entitled, "Cancer: the Forbidden Cures," so that you will understand the depth of this manipulation in the traditional medical model.

Don't be passive in this fight. Recognize your own confinement. Remain empowered and exercise your right to have more. Draw upon a wide array of choices at your disposal to attack the cancer, not your body. You can work within and without the conventional medical model to bolster your chance at living through this illness and finding your way to health again. According to IMS Health, a worldwide leader in health care research, the global market for pharmaceuticals was expected to top 1 trillion in sales by 2014. As former pharmaceutical industry representative Gwen Olson discussed, it's important to recognize that the pharmaceutical industry is not in the business of curing illness. They are focused on symptom control and managing disease. Olson further argues that if they were in the business to cure, they would not be profitable. From 2003-2012, the largest drug companies in the world generated a net profit of 711.4 billion dollars (Drugwatch.com, 2010).

⌘

STEERING CLEAR OF SECONDARY THREATS

CANCER TREATMENTS INVOLVE EXTREMELY dangerous medicines and practices. This is no small matter. It is important to protect yourself and take great care when choosing any proposed treatment protocol.

The statistical death rate for those with cancer seems intimidating enough. However, with an ultimate goal of self-protection, I found thinking about the risk of death or harm from secondary causes to be an effective strategy in my decision making process. In other words, my main goal was to become healthy overall. In my case, I'm sure it took many years to become ill, so I thought, "Why should I expect to heal quickly?"

The expectation that we should kill cancer as fast as we can may lead to harming oneself beyond repair. That is, effects from the chosen treatment and/or surgeries can leave one vulnerable to rapid destruction of quality of life or to succumb to an earlier death. When contemplating treatment, I placed these considerations very high. Anything I thought would put me at high risk for harm in the long run was dismissed as a treatment option. I felt strongly that if I was to truly win the battle, I had to be smart and strategic, remembering thoughtfully that my body needed protecting at all times. That meant attacking the cancer while protecting my body from injury or life-threatening harm.

If treatment kills the cancer but leaves you irreparably damaged, then what is the point? Quality of life is an important issue to consider. Not just saving your life, but considering what that life may look or feel like in the future. Protecting your health and wellbeing as you seek treatment is essential at this time.

Many people with cancer die from secondary causes and not the cancer itself. It is certainly understandable that a doctor may not emphasize the possible side effects or secondary threat to your health that any given treatment may pose. After all, the priority is to clear the body of cancer. Unfortunately, the practices and medicines currently in place to accomplish this carry a wide variety of risks. Prioritizing this knowledge and keeping this in mind when caring for yourself may protect you from great risks or harm to your ultimate health.

While these issues add complexity to the problem at hand, I realized I had to consider self-protection and also the issue of recurrence. If I didn't protect my immunity and if I allowed too much destruction, I thought I would increase my risk of recurrence. I would lose the fight because I took my already struggling body and further attacked its ability to defend against disease.

When we refuse treatments that may be entirely self-destructive like excessive amounts of chemotherapy or radiation, it may actually increase our chances of survival. Protecting the immune system is an integral part of helping the body in its ultimate fight against recurrence. Staving off cancer is the goal and the immune system is the key.

Being self-protective may leave you in a better position to win the first battle and significantly decrease the chances of having to face a second one with cancer. Further, a steady mindfulness on honoring the body's own time frame during the process of healing is an exceptional strategy. Considering these aspects will help you become healthy and will minimize suffering or permanent damage to your health.

⌘

UNDER THE SURFACE

"Be kind. Everyone you meet is in the midst of a great struggle."
—Plato

ON THE DAYS I HAD A SCARF ON, I was obviously sick. Thin, pale and bald: it was apparent I was in peril. If I did go out at all, I noticed a kindness coming from others. People would smile at me and give me courteous nods. They would acknowledge me, yield to my path.

On other days, when I wore a wig, it wasn't so clear that I was fighting for my life. On those days, people would be seemingly in a bad mood, indifferent, or unkind. At first, I thought, "Wow, why is everyone in such a bad mood today?" Then it hit me, as a vulnerable person in peril, people were struck with compassion. Their kindness, which lurked just under the surface, would emerge.

It was sad to experience that in general people are guarded, their compassion masked, wasting opportunity to be loving toward their fellow human beings. We never know what a person is going through. Wouldn't it be wonderful to always remember this and remain open, loving and kind toward others? This is a way to bring healing to others and we have the power to do it.

⌘

PREDICTING OUTCOMES

AT TIMES I HAVE BEEN ABLE TO enjoy the idea that God can do anything. However, to apply that to my own situation often feels unnatural and challenging, because I am only human. I constantly imagine grossly limiting outcomes as solutions to my problems. God's knowledge and abilities are so far beyond what we can imagine that it is sometimes best to let go of any preconceived idea of what can happen for you. Even though I had great faith and hope when I was ill, I made the mistake of planning out two probable scenarios in my head. The first one was that I would die. The other one was that I would be so blessed to live, but go home fearful of recurrence, spending all day, every day fighting the possibility of dormant metastatic cancer cells becoming active. My life would be a constant battle to avoid cancer.

However, I discovered a wondrous scenario: the truth. God released me from cancer on a level I could not have thought possible, a level I could barely comprehend. As God healed me, He simultaneously assured me the cancer would never return. This released me from a weighty burden, a form of bondage, completely. I was ecstatic. The joy of the Lord was all around me and I celebrated. I believed God's promise, the promise of health.

Then shall your light break forth like the morning, and your healing (your restoration and the power of a new life) shall spring forth speedily…

—Isaiah 58:8

Please remember as you go through your healing journey that anything is possible. When you find yourself contemplating or imagining a future, pick a great one. Let go of any limiting, concrete idea, and ask God to fill in the blank that is the life He wants for you, the abundant and joyful life He has promised to give you.

⌘

LYME DISEASE AND CANCER

LYME DISEASE IS AN EPIDEMIC in the United States. Many people suffer from this disease, which masquerades as many other ailments. In fact, 30,000 cases of Lyme disease are reported to the Center for Disease Control (CDC) every year according to the CDC's website. I include Lyme disease in this book as my healing journey revealed that underlying infections might complicate or exacerbate cancer. Many of those who are diagnosed with cancer may have underlying infections for a period of time prior to cancer diagnosis.

When I was six-years-old I had a fever, and experienced flu-like symptoms after a tick embedded itself into my neck. The tick was removed, but at that time, no further treatment was given. I had never really heard of Lyme disease. For years I suffered from stiffness and pain, depression and anxiety, forgetfulness and mood swings. I had allergic reactions to food, specifically sugar and chemical preservatives, and was fatigued all the time.

Throughout my life I went to doctors, including psychologists and neurologists. I had a difficult time recovering from traumas to my body like car accidents and other physical stresses. Although I exercised regularly and had a good diet, I was constantly suffering, but without any diagnosis. None of these doctors ever checked me for viruses or bacteria. I constantly felt blamed for feeling unwell. The simple explanation offered was that my perspective was off, I was overdoing it, or I was just neurotic. I sought help from counselors and therapists. Often when I was with friends, they would ask if I was okay. They often said, "You look like you're in pain." They were right! I hurt all over.

Long after my first cancer diagnosis, approximately twelve months, I tested positive for Lyme disease on the western blot test and through a clinical diagnosis by my doctor. I believe having Lyme for many years either caused or complicated the cancer I had. As my immune system had been challenged for years, it is no wonder I ended up with an inability to fight cancer cells. I was led to what I thought was a cure for cancer which accidentally cured my Lyme disease. This left me feeling stronger than I ever had. Without Lyme disease distracting and challenging my immune system, I was in a much stronger position to battle stage IIIB metastatic uterine cancer. Since my Lyme was cured before my cancer, I call it God's perfect plan for my healing. Indeed, all events and treatments seemed to happen in the right order.

I'm so grateful my doctor tested me for underlying infections after my cancer's recurrence. Doesn't it just seem like good common sense to recognize and treat any infection before you go into battle with cancer? I for one did not or could not expect my immune system to handle such high loads of infections, cancer, and the extreme nature of cancer treatment all at one time. I was at a much higher risk for failure in any treatment plan while having any additional underlying illness.

A reminder, it may be wise to receive a viral panel and western blot test, as well as examine the results before moving forward with treatment decisions. If your treating physician refuses to do these tests or wants to ignore the issue altogether, you may want to go elsewhere for testing and/or treatment. Considering how difficult surgery and cancer treatments are on the body, you may want to lighten the load on your immune system, and clear the body of infection before moving forward.

In my case, surgery was performed before a Lyme diagnosis. Even so, there were indicators or warning signs that something was amiss. A few days after my radical hysterectomy, my doctor commented that I was not healing at the normal rate. No other inquiry was made, just this observation.

Something was clearly wrong with the healing process but no one took the time to investigate. My recovery was extremely difficult because, unbeknownst to me, I was in the process of fighting active Lyme disease. In addition, I was at high risk for recurrence because Lyme is known to communicate with other bacteria, viruses, and cancer cells to activate and proliferate. I interpreted this to mean I probably had zero chance of avoiding recurrence, instead of what studies say to be a 72% chance. This is a marked difference in statistics, and a major difference when fighting for your life.

One main reason I rejected the traditional route of treatment for uterine cancer (not following my regular doctor's recommendations) was because on some deep level I knew I would not survive it. It is imperative to look at the details of one's overall health before and during the battle with cancer. Trust your instincts and get testing done before making decisions about your treatment plan. To learn more about Lyme disease, causes and symptoms, you may start with the resource page of this book and then continue with your own research.

⌘

BEYOND RADIATION

AFTER I COMPLETED TREATMENT THE first time, it became apparent that the bleeding had begun again. At my standard, three-month appointment at USC I expected the exam to go normally, but my doctor announced that she felt something. Stating she was not concerned but wanted to biopsy just to make sure, I agreed. She proceeded to take 25 minutes or so to actually find the smaller than pea-sized lump to biopsy. It was quite painful and I was actually in tears near the end, my tolerance level having been exceeded.

The pathology results revealed metastatic cancer consistent with the form of my original tumor. When I went in to discuss this with my oncologist, she said, "You're not getting out of doing radiation." I did not follow her orders.

It was then that I decided to go to Envita Medical Center in Scottsdale, Arizona for treatment. This treatment center offers integrative medicine and the best of what is offered worldwide. While there, I discovered an option they offered called AAIT, a Natural Killer T-Cell therapy, available in Mexico. This was a process by which they would take a bone marrow sample, approximately 400 ml, and then select the strongest natural killer cells from the group and culture them, growing them to over 10 billion. These would then be re-infused into the body.

I opted to do this while my family and friends worked hard to get the money together. I traveled to Mexico twice, the first time they performed the bone marrow draw and about five weeks later my cells were ready. After I received the cell therapy, I immediately felt my health improve. However, the light bleeding continued. In September I was told to go home and wait three months for the AAIT cells to do their work.

On January 7, 2012 I wrote: "Been home for a couple of months and feeling confident that my cell therapy is working." Then I began bleeding again. I was extremely concerned, but I still wanted to wait for the physical exam from my regular oncologist to evaluate where I was with the cancer. Unfortunately, I contracted the flu, which kept me in bed for over two weeks.

Somewhere around day six of my flu, I became depressed and did not want to do anything to take care of myself. I discontinued my regular practice of making my body a bad host for cancer. After two or three days of this depression I realized I needed to take action, which included considering the possibility that maybe the tumor was not receding. My oncologist was horrified to discover the once pea-sized tumor was now quite large. She could visibly see and immediately palpate what had taken 25 minutes to find just five months prior. She couldn't understand why I had taken an alternative route and felt I had wasted precious time and put my life in jeopardy by going against her advice. I told her everything I had been doing. She wrote it down while shaking her head, then said, "You realize none of this is proven and is all 'experimental' don't you?" I said yes, and went on to explain that I was deeply concerned about long-term effects and damage from radiation. I asked her why she couldn't cut the tumor out. Her answer was that the tumor was too large now and the surgery would be more complicated than I could foresee.

I was perplexed because the first time I asked her to cut it out she said it was too small. She said they wanted to give radiation a chance to work before any further surgery, which was also confusing because it's not typical to be able to do more surgery after radiation, as it damages the tissue so severely that it won't heal properly. So, I was left with her original two options again: radiation for certain and possibly even chemo now. I still wasn't willing to undergo radiation at that time. However, I did agree to see the radiologist for a consultation.

⌘

YOU ARE ENOUGH

I DID NOT RECOGNIZE THAT I WAS in bondage before I became aware of my illness. This bondage was one of the mind in which I was stuck trying to conform to an idea of perfection: an image impressed upon me by the world. This active, never ending and entirely unconscious attempt at conformity led to a detachment from certain parts of myself. I had broken away from various aspects of my uniqueness. This led to an ultimate rejection of the idea that I was enough. What remained was a fragmented version of myself that was unhealthy. My psyche was heavily lacking in self-acceptance. Unfortunately, this was all unconscious until I became aware of my illness and the true need for healing. It is my hope to leave you with a gem of truth that can help you recognize and even restore your fullness. Health comes along with a spiritual wholeness, one that involves self-love and allowing oneself to be embraced by acceptance. In terms of my health, this restoration of self-acceptance, of inviting the fragmented parts of my spirit and psyche to come home, was an integral part of my healing process.

Through this trial, God powerfully shifted my focus to wholeness. I only needed to embrace the person God intended me to be. I was given the wisdom, instilled with a deep knowing, that I am only required to be self-accepting. Through meditation and contemplation, I recognized that was all I had to do to be whole. Wholeness of spirit nurtured by positive thought, self-love, and acceptance would sustain an important aspect of my health, then, now, and always. Through a beautiful connection with the divine, I was reminded that I am never alone, because I am constantly in relationship with a higher power. As I remain aware that Jesus is with me at all times, I may live up to all of God's expectations. The loving, forgiving God does not want me to pressure myself to be my idea of perfect. I am God's idea of perfect because he perfected me in Christ. This is a wonderful truth, which has lifted the immense and continuous pressure I placed upon myself to be other than who I am. Trying to be other than who God made us is not only counterintuitive but it is flat out sad. With our limited understanding of the complexities of our potential we can only diminish our qualities by pigeonholing ourselves into something smaller than what was intended by the divine. This contributes to our own oppression. The oppression I speak of is the conscious or unconscious internalization of oppressive attitudes we perceive or receive from others around us. A time of closeness with God led me to contemplate how He does not want our conformity to worldly ideas. One of His gifts to us is freedom from oppression.

To embrace oneself, seeking only to conform to what God has made you is to become free in wholeness. I had complete gratitude for the gift, the comfort in knowing that we may surpass all worldly expectations by embracing the person God made us, nothing more, and certainly nothing less. This is a real gift, a true freedom. You and I are enough. As we embrace our wholeness, we wait in faith for the gift of restored health. There is no question that God wants us healed.

Beloved, I pray that you may prosper in every way and (that your body) may keep well, even as (I know) your soul keeps well and prospers.

—3 John 1:2

If/when you invite Jesus in, there is healing. Everywhere Jesus went, he healed.

⌘

JOURNAL ENTRIES

FEBRUARY 18-27, 2012

FEBRUARY 18, 2012

I had a shift yesterday. When I went to bed last night I realized I was not feeling sorry for myself anymore. It felt new and I had not recognized that I had been feeling sorry for myself until I was not anymore. I felt completely different in relation to my cancer. I felt bigger than the cancer for the first time. I felt less identified by the cancer. This felt like a much healthier perspective and it had the outcome of lessening my fears. I'm concerned about my white blood cells going down when I get the chemotherapy. I'm hopeful the counts will go right back up and that I will be better off in the long run. I will begin, hopeful the chemotherapy will kill the cancer, which is already robbing my cells of energy.

February 20, 2012

Today was my first Genetically Targeted Fractionated (GTF) chemotherapy appointment. At 10 AM I received a steroid shot to prevent any possible allergic reactions. I was then placed on an IV saline drip, and given an insulin injection. The insulin dropped my blood sugar. When my blood sugar level went down to 70, I was given an IV antibiotic to avoid any infection of my brain. This is because the blood/brain barrier was open at that point. As my blood sugar continued downward I began to get dizzy and was feeling quite spaced out. At 40, I was beginning to see black holes with bright bands of green light moving around. In other words, I was somewhat hallucinating. At this point, blood sugar around 37, I was infused with four chemotherapy drugs. I received one at a time. They all felt a little different and one drug, nicknamed "the red devil" burned terribly. After all the drugs were given, I was handed a sugary drink so that my blood sugar could be brought up to normal as fast as possible. I was also given glucose/vitamin C and one other thing I cannot remember. I opted to get Zoforan for nausea, which I believe helped. I experienced severe stomach cramping after the drink. I did feel my tumor get hot a couple of times which led me to believe the chemo was delivered directly to it, which was amazing.

February 27, 2012

Today I realized that God has been trying to bring me to health for quite a long time. Truly, Lyme disease had been destroying my health for so long, chipping away at my ability to function. Recognizing the cancer had taken hold and was "killing me," long before I realized how bad off I was. To view this as a time of healing only and not a time of illness seems to be more in alignment with what God sees. I feel strongly that God has had His eye on me my entire life and has led me on a journey to health. He is working within me to bring me to full health. This is my healing journey now and I am restored to perfect health and full strength. In Jesus name, I pray, may it be so and let it be! Amen.

⌘

UNSEEN SUPPORT

WHEN I WAS RECEIVING CHEMOTHERAPY, thus extremely ill and yes, at times frightened at the level of suffering I was experiencing, things happened to keep me steadily comforted and deeply touched. Many of these comforts came in the form of dreams. My father had grown up in Key West. I spent time in Florida as a youngster, when the terrain was still cobblestone streets and the landscape lush with various trees. I stayed in the big house on Duval Street where he had lived with siblings, aunts, uncles, and his parents. Over the years I had the pleasure of meeting most of these relatives although I did not make a strong connection with some of the more distant relatives, or so I thought.

One April evening, I dreamt I stood at the front gate of a small house in Key West. I recognized it was my great Aunt Ida's old house that I had visited once or twice in the past. As I arrived, I saw what I thought to be Aunt Ida's daughter Mae. There were two other people there who I did not know, but I sensed they were my kin. All of them positioned themselves around me and embraced me one by one.

They lent their loving support and care, giving it freely and generously. They let me know they were there, perfectly bolstering me up. When I woke, I felt a strength and comfort derived from their loving embraces. The dream led me to imagine I had ancestral support existing beyond my dreams. I was connected to my ancestors who knew I needed them and were there to answer my call. This dream solidified a comfort I already felt from the divine. There was support present beyond what I could see during my daily life. It was there, working in my life, unseen and far beyond any limitations of my imagination. Dreams can be beautiful reminders of an unseen support, existing, permeating, and contributing to our healing path.

⌘

INTERVENTION FROM A PRAYER WARRIOR

ONE DAY, MY SISTER-IN-LAW CALLED from work. She left a message explaining that she had met a woman in the parking lot and told her of the battle I was going through with cancer. This woman Sharice, offered to pray for me and with me via telephone. Even though I was not taking calls at the time, my gut told me I should accept this offer.

After introductions, Sharice began to pray for me. She explained she was using Luke 14. She verbalized many truths. Among them, that I am God's perfect daughter and that He loves me. She commanded that the battle for me be overcome with the good of the Lord and that all the spirits of illness leave me, never to return. Further, she prayed that I be completely free from any insecurity. She informed me that I should always use my mind, thoughts, and words to serve the Lord. She strongly commanded my faithfulness. Sharice reminded me that I was to think God's thoughts after Him. She said I am the daughter of a great King, that He heals me, that Jesus died for me and made me perfect again.

I wrote the following paragraph in my journal just hours after the call.

February 29, 2012

Despite having been so fatigued and unwell, I feel renewed by the power of her belief, by her words. I know I will continue to be healed by the Lord. He is restoring my health now and may accomplish this over a period of time, or in a single moment. I declare that I believe I am healed. The Lord has blessed me today. Through Sharice, I was instructed to stay away from anything that might hinder my relationship with Him. I was left with the understanding that as I am freed of affliction, so will others be.

One gift in having cancer is the profound experience of receiving love from others. They are examples of God's great mercy and love which, when acknowledged, is the greatest gift of all.

⌘

SECOND OPINIONS

AS I SEE AND HAVE EXPERIENCED a grossly limited system in which doctors are only allowed to give specific standardized treatment to those with disease, I cannot see a great value in a second opinion within that same system. This is not to say that dosages or deliveries shouldn't be negotiated. It is only to remind those who are battling for their lives that just because two or more doctors give you the same information, does not mean it is right for you. When I was exploring treatment there really were not that many options offered within the western model. The same drug was offered and the same types of radiation. It gave me no comfort that six doctors recommended either the same or a slight difference in treatment. This did not make me secure in the idea of getting a second opinion. Have confidence in your research. Ask the hard questions. What is the rate of success? What is the chance of creating resistant strains of cancer, or will this kill dormant metastatic cancer cells? What is the risk to my organs and my immune system?

All of these factors play a role in whether or not your treatment will be successful. As far as the radiologist is concerned, ask what type of side-effects you should expect. For example, if you're to get radiation in the upper regions of the body, ask what the percentage risk is of your having to get a feeding tube implanted. What are the long-term risks of losing the function of your salivary glands, your ability to swallow, intake or digest food properly? All of these factors affect your quality of life and also whether or not you survive the damage that is inflicted upon you during treatment. Find confidence in your own common sense opinion, intuition, and research, about how this treatment will help you and affect you long term.

⌘

OUTSIDE THE U.S. BOX: VACCINE IN MEXICO

IT WASN'T UNTIL ABOUT A SIX WEEKS after I started treatment at Envita that I heard about Autogolous Adoptive Immunotherapy (AAIT) of Natural Killer Cells. I inquired about the process and cost. I was happy to hear that unlike other similar treatments offered, the AAIT offered an infusion of natural killer cells, which was similar to a transplant of my own immune system. After hearing the details, I wanted to have the AAIT treatment. In my mind, what better treatment could there be than to utilize and encourage one's own immune system to kill cancer? I had read up on other similar treatments but most of them involved an alteration of the T cell. One example would be the attachment of foreign isotopes to the T cell before reinfusion into the body. I was uncomfortable at the prospect of these alterations and had heard of one specific case where a woman died because of it. She had the unfortunate experience of her lung tissue being attacked by the cells instead of the cancer. Even if I had been interested, the treatments were usually only available through clinical trials. I found out very early on when seeking innovative treatments that they were hardly available to me due to their strict criteria. In conventional medicine, I was not offered anything that involved T cell therapy. Clinical trials may be more easily accessed for those who have a terminal diagnosis in writing.

Not long after I began treatment at Envita, my friend Esha shared why she chose Envita along with a story involving AAIT. She said that while having chemotherapy for metastatic colon cancer at a Canadian hospital, she often received treatment alongside a little girl about age seven. After several rounds, and over a couple years of chemotherapy treatment, there were no other treatment options available through the hospital. She said in her view the girl was in essence "sent home to die." Esha was saddened to say goodbye as she herself remained for more chemotherapy. After many months, Esha was still receiving her treatments when the girl came back in for a follow-up appointment with her oncologist. Far from the look of a dying child, she appeared healthy and was thriving. She was happy, full of life, and her hair was growing back. When Esha asked the parents what had happened, they told her they had taken their daughter to Envita where she received AAIT at their center in Mexico. Little did Esha know, soon she too would be "sent home to die," with her doctor saying, "Well, you should be okay through the summer." Having exhausted most of her options, Esha decided to go to Envita for treatment.

I couldn't imagine how I would be able to receive AAIT due to the cost, I asked God for it and held no doubt in my mind that I would receive it. I spoke with my father about it and within a week or so I was told a friend of my father's had offered to pay for the vaccine. This was an incredible gift and the stakes were too high to say no. As the money was there, we proceeded to plan my first trip to Mexico to get my bone marrow drawn. Here are a few journal entries from my second trip to Mexico when the cells were infused, and my experience with AAIT.

October 10, 2011

I am in Mexico now and just received 1/2 billion out of 20 billion NKT cells. I am feeling a detox effect (sweats, chills and a bit of nausea). The most interesting sensations of heat are moving through my body. It is truly amazing that this is part of my healing journey. I'm here enjoying the ocean in Mexico, accompanied by my sister and beautiful friends, Sheryl and Esha. I have been so deeply encouraged, in fact blessed in following this specific path of healing. Getting to know other patients here and learning their heroic stories in relation to their illnesses is inspirational. Whether they battle cancer, Lyme disease or other autoimmune disorders, they face their limitations with strength and find meaning in their experience. They are all warriors as they fight for health.

The first evening after I received those initial ½ billion cells I felt a distinct sensation in my head. I couldn't really describe it to my sister who was lying in bed with me. I told her it felt really good, similar to carbonation bubbling in my brain. It was very strange to say the least but it didn't frighten me.

October 11, 2011

I received 3 billion NKT cells today, which took a total of about 35 minutes and then was observed for slightly over an hour. I haven't had any issues with feeling sick. The only experience so far is heat in strange places like my kneecaps for example. I get quite tired right after I receive the cells also. I found out today that I have 12 billion cells available and that I will be able to get the extra 2 billion infused.

In the past they only allowed 10 billion even if someone's cells grew to 20 billion. The experience was very pleasant. Even though we were informed we might feel sick, both Esha and I felt quite well. I was extremely tired but Esha was not.

October 12, 2011

Felt lots of heat, which began at the top of my thigh and worked its way down to underneath my kneecaps once again, where is stayed for quite some time. Then it moved down the front of my shins. The main difference I have felt thus far is that upon waking I do not have the feeling of being ill or panicked and anxious. This of course was something I felt on a mental level but seemed to be more from a physical type of exhaustion. This feeling had been there upon waking as far back as I could remember. What an amazement, to wake feeling a lack of illness or physical distress with a relaxed mind.

I looked at the numbers involved and one of the important issues is the cyto-toxicity of the NKT cells, which is the NKT's ability to fight cancer. My cells were rated 16, which is pretty strong. The highest they've seen so far is 20, which was derived from a person who had previously received AAIT. Esha's NKT cells were rated 7.5, which is still not terrible if you consider she received seven years of chemotherapy, which probably caused a lot of damage to her immune system. It's not so far off of 10, which is the minimal preferred level.

To avoid any confusion for those who may choose this treatment in the future, these numbers are no longer used to rate the cells as the process has changed and improved.

⌘

JARED

JARED'S WORDS: "THE LORD HAS NEVER FAILED ME." He knew he had more to do here. "God is depending on our Faith. If our earthly parents are willing to bless us imagine how much our Heavenly Father wants to bless us."

Jared knew in August of 2011 something was seriously wrong. He felt a hard mass. He decided to try to take care of his own health issue by changing his lifestyle a bit, but things progressed. After going for a physical exam required by his employer he was told he had a hernia that required immediate attention. The initial doctor then referred Jared to a urologist who performed an ultrasound and ordered blood work. Results revealed advanced testicular cancer in July 2013. The cancer had started locally in the right testicle and spread to the abdomen and pelvis. The urologist informed him that the cancer was "incurable." An orchiectomy surgery was performed in March followed by four rounds of chemotherapy. Unfortunately the chemotherapy had little effect and caused minimal shrinkage to the tumors.

When I first met Jared he had undergone conventional treatment for two types of cancer. He hated to poison his body but felt he had no choice in the matter. In May, after conventional treatments proved ineffective, he sought help at Envita. There he received immunotherapies and GTF chemotherapy. He was also undergoing radiation (tomotherapy), which had in essence liquefied a large tumor near his abdominal area. Unfortunately, his cancer continued to grow and spread rapidly. A PT scan revealed it had spread to his lung and lymph nodes and a new tumor had appeared on his neck.

At this time conventional medicine offered him the option of three, five-day rounds of chemotherapy followed by two more rounds with a stronger chemotherapy combined with stem cell therapy. Each chemo protocol would include at least five days of hospitalization with 24-hour delivery of the chemotherapy. There were several reasons Jared did not want to undergo this treatment. One, the treatment was said to only be palliative care, with a less than 10% chance of the drug being effective.

Many people including patients at Envita were troubled by Jared's circumstance and prayed he would heal. With things looking so grim it seemed he would inevitably be defeated. Although I could see some people believed Jared would die, many remained hopeful. He received a lot of prayer while in the hospital and had a huge support network of people who prayed for him. He remained hopeful and was extremely patient. He didn't want to rush into anything that would further damage his immune system.

Jared was encouraged to seek treatment at the regular hospital again. He was entirely against it at first. Then, after speaking with two people who spoke the same words about trying it, he felt a sense of peace come over him and recognized the advice as divine guidance.

He checked himself in to receive the first five-day round of chemo.

Jared went through two or three rounds of this protocol. There were complications each time that involved infections and also there was the problem of a wound that would not heal from his initial surgery. Due to the complications Jared was not able to go in for his fourth round of chemo protocol. But, miraculously, Jared's PT scan came up clear soon after his third round in January of 2015.

Jared had some dead tissue (previously a cancerous tumor) in his abdominal area near a main artery in the leg. This was dangerous as it was an open wound with gangrenous infection. This wound caused pain and would not heal. After countless consultations and talk about surgery to remove the tissue, this option was ruled out as a possibility. He was referred to what was supposedly the best wound clinic in the country where he received a consultation. I spoke with him after his visit to those doctors. He said they hadn't even really reviewed his chart. They came into the room and said, "What can we do for you?" The two doctors offered to amputate his leg and hip (hemipelvectomy), stating it was necessary to get rid of the cancer. They kept insisting there was cancer present, even after Jared told them the tissue had been biopsied several times and only revealed pyoderma gangrenosa. Jared refused the surgery despite being told there was no other solution and the wound that would never heal posed a threat to his life.

He is one more example of a lie neutralized. It is also a story of someone exercising self-protection in the face of fear. He was told he had no other option; that he had to face a life with no leg and maybe half a pelvis. He decided to take matters into his own hands. Despite the damage from radiation and gangrenous infection, he was able to protect himself from harm. Flash forward three weeks, after tending to his wound, it began to heal. He soaked it with vinegar and water, put a healing salve on it and used other healing agents, like colloidal silver spray. Today, his wound is about 70% healed and this 42-year-old still enjoys the use of his legs.

⌘

AN OUNCE OF PREVENTION

THE PHRASE, "AN OUNCE OF PREVENTION is worth a pound of cure," has been around for a long time. Unfortunately it is no longer true. These days an ounce of prevention is only worth an ounce of cure. Our daily habits will greatly affect our health in the future. With all of the exposure to toxic chemicals, electromagnetic radiation (which is doubling every year), xeno-hormones, nuclear fallout, oil spills, pesticides, additives in our food supply, along with molds, fungus, parasites, and high levels of mercury in our fish, it is no wonder it takes more to steer clear of illness. These efforts come in many forms but should include consistent health building activities. Without good habits, it is nearly impossible to be or stay well. By eating a good diet you can stave off all types of problems, which would leave you vulnerable to health crises such as cancer. Whether you have cancer now or not, it is the right time to start building a bridge to health. It is easy to become overwhelmed when deciding on new ways to take care of yourself. However, if you do have cancer now, it is imperative to shift all habits toward great health. In general, it may be wise to avoid health-ruining items such as cigarettes, caffeine, alcohol, carbonated drinks, sugar substitutes (made from chemicals), and excessive amounts of refined sugar. All of these items destroy health on many levels, and weaken your immune system. To avoid problems with weight, insulin resistance, cortisol levels, hormone balance, et cetera, a good diet is essential.

Instead of making this complicated, a simple way to be healthy is to eat real food. That is, organic foods in their natural state. Nothing processed. If you are going to eat meat, organic is the way to go. Cook the meat without any oil. Most heated oils when consumed interfere with your cells ability to breath; they suffocate. In addition, when meat is cooked with oil on the grill, broiler, or frying pan, the oil mixes with the muscle and creates carcinogens. Make your own salad dressings to avoid rancid oils, additives and hydrogenated fat.

When cooking with oil, research the level of heat that particular oil can remain stable at. Heating oil beyond the point of stability makes it toxic. Stay away from all hydrogenated oils, monosodium glutamate, dyes, peanuts, peanut butter, and corn, as they tend to have mold. Once certain foods are avoided, it becomes apparent that real food is all that is left to consume. That is key. Although I don't feel it is always necessary to become a vegetarian, I do recommend reading "Natures First Law: The Raw Food Diet" by Stephen Arlin, as it changes the perspective on how to look at your body and food consumption in general. Simply stated, think of feeding your cells and not your gut when you eat. How is the food you eat going to be easily digested and readily delivered to your cells?

Switch from table salt to Himalayan salt. Limit the amount of prescribed or over-the-counter medicines you take. These are all chemicals and create toxicity in the body. Since it is impossible to entirely avoid toxins and chemicals, it is wise to take Epsom salt baths weekly, and detox in saunas or find a way to sweat daily. The detoxifying of heavy metals would require testing and chelation, but spirulina and chlorella can bind to heavy metals and help to bring them out of the system. Lastly, to avoid foods that cause inflammation in the body is a good idea, like wheat and dairy. Turmeric may bring down inflammation.

Look for natural alternatives to any medication you are currently taking. One example is switching from over the counter allergy medications to Allerplex by Standard Process or another homeopathic remedy for allergy relief. Flush your liver of toxins daily by drinking lemon in water in the mornings. There are many books on health but I encourage you to become sensitive to how foods make you feel. Hold foods or drinks in your hand and then contemplate, "Does this make me feel weak or does it make me feel strong?" If the answer is weak, then avoid that food at least for that day. Of course, I am not a doctor. In my opinion though, these changes were essential for my healing to occur.

⌘

YOUR INHERITANCE

IN MY EXPERIENCE, THE CHURCH failed to empower me by neglecting to teach in depth about the Holy Spirit. This in effect, deprived me of an important understanding of what I inherited from Jesus. When I was going through some of my darkest days, incredibly ill from the chemo and thinking I might die from either the treatment or the cancer, I prayed continuously. I trusted God with my future, one held in the palm of His hand. After I was recovering from the chemo it became boldly apparent that God wanted me to know that I, as a believer, had spiritual authority given to me because I inherited it from Christ, and that Christ abides in me. The true meaning of "I in He and He in me" is a full description of our inheritance, which includes freedom from oppression and deliverance from affliction.

Jesus is within us and we are in Him. We can be assured that God's promises are real. Thus, no need to believe or act as if Jesus has not already fulfilled his perfect sacrifice. The results or consequences of this play out here, now, in the reality of our lives. It is disempowering to lack a good understanding of the Holy Spirit.

What are some of these rights and spiritual authorities, which can also be described as responsibilities (the following of God's commandments)? First, we have prayer, praying in line with the Holy Spirit or Intercessory prayer. Second, we have the authority to perform deliverance, casting out all roots of darkness from ourselves, and our families in the name of Jesus. Third, we have the very real, spiritual practice of being steadfast in faith, that is, continual belief in Him. Fourth, we have the sword of the Spirit, which is the word of God. In essence, all is done according to your faith in Him. We have faith that all of God's promises are real, that He fulfills them. We command God's promises by believing in them with all of our hearts and minds. Giving thanks is another active way to praise God and stay in communion with Him.

Why is this important for you to know? My answer is because now is the time when you are vulnerable and have succumbed to illness. You are weakened by disease in your body, mind, and spirit. To abide in the truth is to live within the light of God and to be protected from harm. To practice all of these things is to be active in exercising your spiritual authority. You utilize your inherited gifts by doing all of these things. As you put on the full armor of God, evil schemes are demolished. As you remain connected to divine power, fully submitted to God, the Holy Spirit is the one who communicates with you. He helps you to make correct choices during this trial. The battle for you will be won because you have faith and abide in the truth. As God is the author of creation, His commandments apply to how reality works. This is why when we follow commandments, we experience and receive life, as it should be. Ask and it is given applies to your reality. In Him, "we live and move and have our being" (Acts 17:28).

When I laid down for a nap after praying and praising God for all of His promises, all He has given me, including afflictions and pain; I heard God say, "Ask and it will be given you." This became a strong message in the days that followed. This was a communication from the Holy Spirit who reveals scripture to us as it applies to our situation. Remember, He is our helper. So, I asked for the following.

"Lord, I ask for all you have promised me, that your will be done on earth as it is in heaven. I ask to be indwelled by the Holy Spirit who was sent after Jesus departed. I ask for health, knowledge and abundant life. I ask for your love and comfort, for strength to do all that is mine to do. I ask for freedom and mercy. I ask you Lord for all promises that I inherited through Christ's sacrifice and resurrection. I ask to receive, understand and utilize my full inheritance. I ask for my family to be healed. Additionally, I hold faith that I will receive all of God's promises. I understand and acknowledge all I have asked for has been given to me, even if I don't see it yet, even if I have not experienced it yet, in Jesus name I pray, Amen."

Paul speaks of the power of those who believe, thus this applies to you, the hope-filled being.

For this reason, because I have heard of your faith in the Lord Jesus and your love toward all the saints, I do not cease to give thanks for you, remembering you in my prayers, that the God of our Lord Jesus Christ, the Father of glory, may give you the Spirit of wisdom and of revelation in the knowledge of Him, having the eyes of your hearts enlightened, that you may know what is the hope to which He has called you, what are the riches of His glorious inheritance in the saints, and what is the immeasurable greatness of

His power toward us who believe, according to the working of His great might that He worked in Christ when he raised him from the dead and seated him at his right hand in the heavenly places, far above all rule and authority and power and dominion, and above every name that is named, not only in this age but also in the one to come.

—Ephesians 1: 15-21

You may ask at any time to have the eyes of your heart opened. Ask Jesus to grant you the spirit of wisdom and of revelation in the knowledge of Him, to know exactly what decisions to make on your healing path. Praise Him that you may bask in His light. You have been given a future and a hope. Remember and believe it has been given to you.

⌘

WHAT IS MY NAME?

IT IS APRIL 5, 2012, AND I'M GOING for immunotherapy at Envita. Last night I studied John 20 and Revelations 21. It was timely as this is Holy Week and it was Ash Wednesday yesterday. I'm looking forward to going to church on Easter and celebrating the resurrection of our Lord and Savior. Last night I commanded spirits of any affliction and infirmity to come out of me in the name of Jesus.

Recently on March 30th, two ladies, Marilyn and Florence had prayed for me for 20 minutes. There was a point when Marilyn began to call me "Michelle" instead of Nicole. As she went on to refer to me as Michelle, I did not want to interrupt her prayer. She then went back to calling me Nicole as she had done earlier and continued to correctly use my name as she closed.

After the prayer, Marilyn told me that images or ideas might come to my mind's eye in the days that followed their prayers. Marilyn encouraged me to pay attention to these images and what they revealed. She instructed that God might bring issues up for healing in this manner and I need not get anxious but simply observe and then ask Jesus what needs to be done about the matter, if anything.

Being quite ill and mostly bedridden, I often had severe panic and fear. I felt physically and mentally traumatized from the chemo drugs. I always battled those feelings with prayer. Tonight was no different. While trying to fall asleep, I had fear come upon me, so I began to pray and fell into a light sleep. A few minutes later as I awakened, images came up on the blank screen of my mind's eye. I saw quick flashes of myself; the first picture, a reflection of my appearance in the recent past, before my hair fell out. Then what followed, an image of myself wearing a blonde wig, then again, another picture of myself wearing a brown wig. The "show" ended with an image of myself bald, which conveyed a stripping of my identity. Just then, I heard the name Michelle called out. My immediate reaction was to ask, "Do I need to change my name?" I answered myself thinking, no because I knew my name was not supposed to be Michelle.

Surely, God was revealing this to me for a reason and I decided to await an answer about whether or not additional attention should be paid to this issue.

During this time I experienced being readily led by God. I felt I was communicated with and instructed on what to do quite often. The next morning after waking, God told me to go and take Holy Communion, and I made plans to do so. I was too ill to go that Sunday morning and was barely able to make the evening service. I took Holy Communion and felt somewhat embarrassed, as I had to sit during the entire message because I was so weak. After the service, I spoke with the Priest. My mother was there and we shared a bit about my ordeal with cancer and of course, the recent miracle I had received. During the conversation, after the priest had correctly called me

Nicole, he began to use the name Michelle. I took notice of this and did not correct him. He then reverted back to calling me Nicole. This stood out again and reminded me of times in the past when people called me Michelle. It was practically a life theme for about seven years. I wondered why it was happening again. Confusion around my name was once again being revealed to me. Honestly, I don't think I would have paid such attention to the misuse of my name had it not been called out by only the Holy people I was coming into contact with and at this important time in my life.

I reflected back to the many times when people who had known me for years would begin to call me Michelle. Clearly they knew my name but somehow they were unable to stop calling me Michelle. For example, A co-worker of over three years came into the office one day and said, "Good morning Michelle, how are you today?" I said, "Do you mean Nicole?" He felt embarrassed, saying he knew my name. This occurred for a few months and finally, we talked about it. He said he just did not know what had come over him; it was like he had no control over calling me by the wrong name, that certainly he knew my name was Nicole. Wouldn't you know the very next morning he came in and said, "Hi, good morning Michelle," and smiled. I smiled back and thought, "Is he kidding?" Again, he realized what he had said, sat down in a chair, put his head in his hands, shook his head saying, "I just can't stop calling you Michelle!"

⌘

RAYMOND

MY MOTHER AND I WERE AT THE Kierland Hotel in Scottsdale when we ran into Raymond. He was a bellman at the hotel whom we had met two months prior. We had a couple nice conversations with him. As my mom and I both approached him at once, I realized he might not recognize me but he may recognize my mother. I asked, "Do you remember Karen?" Then my mom asked him, "Are you Raymond?" After we both spoke, he recognized my voice. All of the sudden he was familiar with us and said he did remember us. My mom asked him, "Remember the last time you saw us, Nicole asked you, 'Okay Raymond, now are you going to recognize me if I lose all my hair?'" It all came flooding back to me and I giggled.

Even though I really did not believe I would lose my hair this made me think maybe I really did know it would happen. My mom told him of the miracle I had and I told him that women had prayed for me and the cancer died within two days, over the weekend. After hugging me twice, he began to share his story with us.

His mother had passed from breast cancer two years earlier. I asked what her name had been. "Wilma," he said and then shared with us that it had taken him 40 years to understand her. He said that Wilma had come from a high- class family in Jamaica and so had been completely marginalized after getting pregnant and having a child out of wedlock. All of Wilma's siblings and the rest of her family had alienated her, pressured her, and disapproved of her from a young age. However, Raymond realized after her death, that his mother had been given a gift due to this life challenge, and that his mother developed a very strong, true and stable identity as a child. I said, "Oh, you mean, she was free!" He said, "Yes! She had the freedom," I finished his sentence, "to embody wholeness." He replied, "That's right, that's the exact right word."

Raymond continued sharing that when he came to the United States, he changed his last name to his mother's maiden name because he recognized he was coming here as he was: a whole person who was unashamed and unapologetic. He realized by embracing his name, his wholeness, he too was free. Free to not conform to anyone else's idea of who he should be. Free to be completely true to himself. Raymond realized then, there was nothing else he had to do. I high fived him and told him that this was the understanding I had been brought to just days earlier.

I knew I had been reborn, and had become a person who accepted herself completely. I was now an unapologetic woman, a woman who embraced her own wholeness and was no longer willing to cut off from parts of herself to fit in or avoid rejection or anything else in life. This completely freed me to realize that I need do nothing else. I only have to do this and rely on grace, as the divine loves me unconditionally. To serve Him, to be whole, to be prosperous, to be anything at all, I just needed to know my name. What an utter blessing and freedom to know my name, to be "me." I was excited Raymond shared the story with me. Where two people agree, let it be so. Little did I know at that time, I was about to get a new name also!

⌘

GOD-GIVEN NAME

I DECIDED TO SPEAK WITH MY MOM about the images that had come to mind and about people calling me Michelle. As she came to check on me one early morning I spoke with her about the ladies and the priest. She chimed in immediately, saying, "I know exactly what it is. They are picking up on the 'm' sound in your name, because I chose the name Micol when I was pregnant with you." Some family members had expressed a strong dislike to it, so she squashed her desire to give me the name. She ended up choosing "Nicole," because it was similar. She expressed this was not the name that was in her heart; she was young at the time and did not know anyone else by that name. Right as my mom shared this, I knew that God was leading me to claim my true name. I expressed joy to my mother and told her that I would claim my name on that very day.

To name something is to take dominion over it. My name change came along with a reminder of the truth. How personally God cares for me, that He desired for me to have my true name, and it mattered. I believe God has delivered me again. I feel like a newborn babe, my name intact and all of my birthrights renewed. I stand in wholeness.

⌘

POWER OF THE HOLY SPIRIT

I WRITE NOW ABOUT THE HOLY SPIRIT as you are in the battle for your health. The battle for health includes spiritual elements, thus it is also a spiritual battle. As you listen for truth and direction on your healing journey, this is the voice that communicates to you. This voice played an imperative role in my healing so I share this with you in the hopes you have an ear to listen for direction.

But the Helper, the Holy Spirit, whom the Father will send in My name, He will teach you all things, and bring to your remembrance all things that I said to you.

—John 14:26 (ESV)

I asked the Lord to allow me to pray for people with the Holy Spirit. I asked Jesus saying, "I will now pray for (name) and I ask you Lord that I pray in line with the Holy Spirit." What I experienced was that in my mind's eye I saw and felt a powerful force. I understood in that moment a power that could move mountains. I understood how physical things could be affected by this power. This is the power that is promised to all believers in Christ: the power of the Holy Spirit is the power of God. I share this experience with you now for a purpose. It is important that you know that there is a power you receive as a believer that is beyond all other principalities, might and authority, above any other dominion. It is because there is no greater power than the Holy Spirit residing within you, that you have the authority to command your healing. It is because the Holy Spirit rested upon you and now resides in you that you are able to be effective in your own life and in the lives of others. You do this by remaining hopeful and steadfast in the true knowledge that this awesome being, the Holy Spirit that dwells in you, will be your true guide at every step. The Holy Spirit is the communicator, the voice that will lead you down the best path on your healing journey. This is not just the healing of your physical body; it is a deepening in your relationship with the Holy Spirit. You are learning to keep your mind clear and free from worry. You are learning to trust that this communication is the reason you can hear why you should make specific choices, taking one thing and leaving another. This is the voice that keeps you from darkness and on track during this trial in your life. In the chapter "No Prayer Goes Unnoticed," the story I was reminded of after I asked for guidance, Abraham and Isaac, came directly from the Holy Spirit. This is because the Holy Spirit reminds us of things God has said in the past. He provides us with remembrances so that we may have understanding.

And the Spirit of the Lord shall rest upon him, the Spirit of wisdom and understanding, the spirit of counsel and might, the spirit of knowledge and the fear of the Lord.

—Isaiah 11:2 (ESV)

Rest assured, the Holy Spirit is with you now and through eternity, He will never leave you, He is your continual source of divine intelligence and guidance.

⌘

IMAGINATIVE AND THOUGHTFUL SUPPORT

I SAW A TELEVISION SHOW ONCE featuring twelve people who had achieved financial success after having a passion for something in their life. I watched intently wondering what all these people held in common.

They were vastly different and each had attempted various endeavors. Within 30 minutes I heard the common thread. Every one of these people had a support system. Beyond that, their support systems were comprised of friends who provided a very specific kind of assistance. This type of support lived in their minds, thoughts, and beliefs. Indeed every one of those "successful" people shared relationships with people who held the same vision for their success. Whatever they believed for themselves was a shared vision. Others believed the same on their behalf. We have the ability to help each other by holding the idea of health for one another.

If you have cancer, it will benefit you to advise others to share in your belief that you are in a process of healing, and that you will achieve it.

Ask your friends and family members to imagine the best possible outcome for you. In fact, you may want to ask those around you to "see you as healthy" in their mind's eye and in their prayers.

Often I hesitate to tell others I've had cancer in the past because I wish to overcome the label. I don't believe it is healthy to have others picturing or imagining that I may have a recurrence instead of confidently viewing me as a healthy individual. This has not stopped me from sharing my story but I do hold it as a consideration. If or when I see a person "thinking it" and not "saying it," I proceed to tell them how confident I am in my health and why I have no fear of recurrence. In doing this, I hope to coach them out of the typical reactionary belief system that occurs most often in the face of this information. Belief is a powerful thing. Holding faith, hope, and belief in what we cannot see, allows what is there waiting just under the surface, to emerge.

It is your right to remain quiet about your cancer, specifically around those who you feel may label you as ill. However, it may also be a good option to suggest to others what you believe and ask them to hold that vision for you as well.

When someone asks how they can help you, let them know they can lend appreciated and powerful support in this way, by imagining and encircling you in healthfulness. Request they fight alongside you with active thoughtfulness in the battle for your health. Have victory now by celebrating your health in your belief and imagination, before it becomes evident in the physical world.

⌘

A DAY AND A DANCE

MARCH 30, 2012

Today was a wonderful day, the first time in two years I arrived at Envita cancer free. I went in wearing a blue peacock designed dress. Mom had purchased the dress at a store while waiting for me to complete the PT scan the day before. The dress reminded us both of my grandmother Vera who always loved peacocks and painted images of them often. We shared the opinion the dress was a significant reminder that I had my deceased grandmother's support. I was welcomed into Envita by all the beautiful women that worked there. Out front, when Sigrun saw me, she came through the doors and did a victory dance as she moved toward me to give me a huge congratulatory hug. She said, "Well done!" Everyone was so excited. Craig, who I haven't been able to bring myself to speak too because I had been so fatigued and ill, was across the room. As I sat on the couch, I waved to him and smiled asking if he had heard the news. He smiled and said yes. He was so happy for me and gave me the thumbs up. Kim came to get me for treatment and she was thrilled also. Next,

Vicki walked by and when she saw me, presented a beautiful smile. She too gave me such a loving hug; she was just ecstatic I could tell. Then Amanda came in and congratulated me and said they all need the encouragement at the office because people come in there as a last resort often after they have been pummeled with chemo and radiation and their immune systems have been so wrecked that it is often difficult to then turn it around. I am so grateful to have gone to Envita for treatment early on, in the beginning. The difficulty of accepting that I had to undergo chemotherapy and radiation was eased by Envita's methods. I struggled and worked hard to accept that I was guided to do chemo and radiation because I was so wholly afraid and against it for so long. However, God told me that was what I needed to do. I was grateful that Envita offered a specialized type of chemo, and found a solution so I could receive targeted radiation.

After treatment mom and I met with the doctor who went over the results of PT scan. It stated there was one spot that was suspicious for recurrence however there was no evidence of tumor and the doctor said of course they were reading it as the beginning of something when we all know that it is indeed the end. There was a tumor there that was approximately and inch and a half in diameter and radius, and now nothing. I'm so thrilled and still trying to wrap my head around this new freedom and joy God has given me with this miracle.

Exact notation on the PT scan results, March 29, 2012:

1. A focal hotspot in the vaginal cuff in the left is worrisome for local recurrence.
2. There is no measurable mass.
3. No specific evidence for distant metastasis elsewhere.

⌘

ESCORTED HOME

ON THE DAY MY SISTER AND I headed back home to L.A., we had an escort. A biker looking just like a character in a movie pulled up alongside us. He waved at us and said hello after moving ahead of us on the road. At some point, after ten minutes, he signaled us to slow down. Clearly we were protected from receiving a speeding ticket from a nearby highway patrol officer. I realized at some point that he was our own personal escort and another living example of how God provides us with what we need. I was actually having a difficult day, as I was worried about the long drive and not having any energy. Having an escort lifted my spirits and encouraged me to push ahead.

⌘

A KIND GESTURE

NOT LONG AFTER I HAD COMPLETED chemotherapy, approximately five months later, I was able to take a trip to Kauai. This trip had been planned almost a year in advance. I had low expectations of being able to make it there. Although I was weak and bald, I went ahead, toting with me a heightened awareness that life may be shorter than once imagined. I was determined to enjoy time with my family.

One day at the hotel, my mom and I gazed at the blue ocean while sitting beneath two yellow umbrellas. A waiter came by to take our drink orders. As he jotted them down, he asked how we were doing. I replied saying we're wonderful, just appreciating this moment, the fact that we're alive. At least 40 minutes had passed since I requested a pineapple juice. I finally gave up on the drink idea and wondered over to a distant restroom. Ten minutes later I returned to find the iced drink placed by my chair. After we enjoyed those drinks, the waiter came by, crouched down beside me, and said something to this effect: "We have a lot in common because I can appreciate the gift of each breath also. Every moment is a blessing. You deserve to be here.

Congratulations and well done."

I realized later that waiter hit on a very meaningful issue. On some very deep unconscious level as a sick person, I held a false belief that I was not deserving, somehow not good enough, for this world. This left me to wonder if other people with cancer have some underlying sadness, a lack of surety that they indeed deserve to be here. If any part of us accepts that lie, it can be a threat to our lives.

Nothing could be further from the truth, and of course during my healing process, the part of me that felt unworthy did come to light and received healing. The part of me that believed the lie of unworthiness died instead of me.

⌘

HEIGHTENED SENSES

MY MOM AND I WENT OUT AND got massages one night. After we parked at the hotel, we got out of the car and started walking through the parking lot. We were greeted by the sound of a Top 40 song, and kids playing. Then we saw beautiful flowers: white, purple, and red. I danced through the lot and was weeping with joy. I ran my hands over the flowers and was so touched at the gift of life and all that was happening around me.

We got to the counter at the spa, where I saw Easter eggs with a sign that read: Open an egg and receive 5–20 % off Pive products. I asked the cashier what Pive products were, and she said they were hair products. I laughed out loud and said, "That's the one thing I don't need right now," thinking of my hairless head covered by a scarf. The massage was wonderful and healing.

On the way out we passed the flowers and there was still a beautiful breeze. All I could smell was the glorious smell of those flowers that permeated the air! I told my mom in the relaxation room, while awaiting our massage, "That's the best music I've ever heard and those were the prettiest flowers I had ever seen."

⌘

AFTERMATH

I WENT HOME TO REST AND RECOVER from my long battle with cancer. I had gone through months of deep suffering and fighting fear. During my battle, I felt the threat of death, and some of the treatments I experienced represented a major physical assault. After returning home "cured" I tried to get my feet back on the ground and go back to functioning as a healthy person would. It takes a lot of time to feel better once you've been walking the razor's edge between life and death. I can't remember when it all started, but I began to have new fears. These fears were anxieties about great physical harm coming to me in different ways. For example, while taking a shower I would imagine an earthquake that would throw me against the glass shower door. Another common fantasy occurred while driving: I would imagine what it would feel like to get crushed by an oncoming truck.

After over a month of these recurring thoughts, I recognized this was not normal. These troublesome ideas were having a negative effect on my daily life. It seemed I was suffering from some type of anxiety disorder, and I decided to seek counseling for the symptoms.

There are many symptoms that may occur if you have

posttraumatic stress. My own anxiety about getting physically injured was not the only symptom I experienced but it was very severe. I think the problems came from some of the treatments that caused me great pain and trauma, and the idea that we may all have a healthy denial of our own vulnerability, which is fragile and can be broken down by a traumatic event. To become so keenly aware of my fragility partnered with physical pain and suffering, was too much for my psyche to bear. It took time to rebuild a healthy denial of my own physical weaknesses, and to forget the pain.

It has come to light that many patients who go through surgery and other treatments face these types of disorders. Posttraumatic Stress Disorder (PTSD) is an anxiety disorder that develops after a traumatic event. There is another disorder closely related to PTSD called Acute Stress Disorder. Whatever the name, it's a good idea to watch for signs and get help if necessary to work through it. Research is easily done online to find out how to get counseling for your specific needs.

⌘

WHAT ABOUT HORMONES?

IT'S DIFFICULT TO SAY THAT I REGRET surgery because I'm alive and that is the outcome of all of my choices. However, I would say I regret having not put enough thought into the matter. In some ways I feel I was a victim of what I warn against, rushing into something because you believe it is necessary for survival. Looking back, I would have considered more thoughtfully what this surgery would mean for my future quality of life. Also, I would have put more restrictions and boundaries on my surgeon as to what she could and could not do during the procedure.

The Surgery lasted over five and a half hours with 42 of my lymph nodes removed along with my ovaries, ovarian tubes, cervix, and uterus. I was cut first with four smaller incisions to allow a laparoscopic attempt to deliver my uterus vaginally. This failed after a couple of hours of surgery and ultimately I was cut vertically over my belly button. If I had to do it over again I would have at least limited the ways they could cut me and I would absolutely tell the surgeon she was not to take so many of my lymph nodes. I wasn't given many specifics during my consult for surgery. I was told it was necessary to try to save my life and only informed that some of my lymph nodes would be checked for cancer. I have since learned that taking your lymph nodes compromises your immunity and also can cause edema, which can be quite problematic.

My recovery was long and painful. It took about five months to be able to walk up the block. I was left with a body that could not produce any hormones, and all the symptoms of a surgically induced menopause. After a couple of weeks without hormones, I began having severe hot flashes which included a wave of extreme nausea, heart racing, anxiety, and then an extreme release of heat followed by a freezing cold chill. All of this happened over a two minute interval, every five minutes or so.

This went on for a long time. The frequency and severity diminished after a year of extremely good eating habits (a cancer diet). When the symptoms subsided I felt I was all right for the moment. This all fell apart after my first chemotherapy infusion. There I was again having intense hot flashes, which was awful. When I returned home after healing from cancer I was living a life of suffering from lack of hormones, but could not take any to relieve my symptoms.

I had an estrogen receptor positive (estrogen fed) aggressive cancer and it was the advice of doctors not to receive any hormone therapy. My heart raced frequently and at night my heart would beat really hard. My DHEA levels were that of a 70-year-old. Due to this, I could not build muscle and I could see changes in my skin and hair. My sexuality was completely gone. I had vaginal atrophy, which is shrinkage of the vaginal canal and thinning of the lining of the vaginal wall. This was extremely painful and lubricants did not work to alleviate the pain. I suffered for over two years before I finally decided to go ahead and seek out bio identical hormones.

I researched hormone replacement therapy as much as I was able. I struggled a lot with the decision to take hormones because certainly I would not want to get cancer again, but I weighed that risk with my quality of life and my specific circumstance. I went to another OBGYN who was willing to give me a very low dose of progesterone and estrogen. I read several studies and also thought about the risks of not having hormone therapy, i.e. bone loss, deterioration of my colon and bladder, heart attack, or stroke.

I didn't receive a lot of support for getting hormone therapy. Most of my family worried for me. The doctor at Envita wanted to do more research but he didn't feel comfortable with it either. I met a patient at Envita who had opted to take hormone therapy due to similar reasons. She was getting treatment for cancer again, because her cancer had returned within a year of taking hormone therapy. She told me she wouldn't do it again. She encouraged me to stop taking the hormones. My father also wanted me to quit. He said anything is better than having cancer again.

I also hated to lie to my oncologist but I feared her response. When she saw my lining of the vaginal canal was healthier, she asked me what I was doing. I admitted I was taking a small amount of progesterone. She was very unhappy and asked why I was doing it. I replied that I was in too much pain to continue without it. She reiterated that taking hormones would elevate my risk of recurrence. This statement terrified me as it always had in the past but I still am using hormones to this day. I'm finally able to build muscle again and all the pain is gone. I sleep at night and my heart is beating regularly again. Age 41 was just too early to start with bone density loss and all the other problems that came with a lack of hormones.

I certainly am not a doctor and I am not recommending that others do what I have done. I share this only because it is one more example of my not allowing fear to steer my choices. I've had to stave off the fear of an imminent return of cancer to protect my overall health and wellbeing. I view hormone replacement therapy as a type of supplement that my body is lacking and does not function well without.

⌘

GIFTS REVEALED

THERE WASN'T JUST ONE GIFT I found through this journey of healing, but many. First, the amazing outpour of love I experienced from friends and family. The love I received from strangers. The close bonds I formed with those beautiful people I met along the way. Second, I was presented with an opportunity to spiritually change, and grow. Third, the dream, inspiration and assignment to write "Hope Over Fear". Fourth, the formation of my non-profit organization, Cancer Warrior Inc. Fifth, to experience a much deeper level of communion with God. To know His love so surely, so intimately that I could never deny His comfort. Ultimately, the great meaning of hope taken from my healing journey and the distinct opportunity to walk in the world whole, healed, truly knowing the warrior within has not only awakened but also emerged.

⌘

WHAT NEXT?

THE MIRACULOUS INTELLIGENCE THAT assists the weak may bring us out of fear and into hope. In that hope, in the light, we will overcome oppressive thoughts and support one another. In hope, we get off of our knees and fight for others the way we just fought to save our own lives. I believe this is part of God's plan for all of us.

I am left inspired by Philippians 4:8-9 (NIV), "Finally, brothers, whatever is true, whatever is noble, whatever is right, whatever is pure, whatever is lovely, whatever is admirable—if anything is excellent or praiseworthy—think about such things. Whatever you have learned or received or heard from me, or seen in me—put it into practice. And the God of peace will be with you."

⌘

The Promise of Health

⌘

Hope Over Fear Workbook

Understanding Medical Models

Taking a look at the differences in Eastern and Western Medicine may be useful while considering which treatments are proposed to you, and by whom. It could greatly benefit you to view your body and disease as defined by the Eastern Medicine and utilize Western Medicine in part, as you see fit. For example, perceiving your body as an ecosystem may lead you to be more protective of the entire body. This concept gives rise to an honoring of the body and all the complexities of protecting it as you endeavor to become well.

Key Differences

Awareness and use of bio-energy or Qi (chi, prana, life force) in the East, unawareness of it in the West. From this flows all the remaining differences: definitions of health, illness, and symptoms, the model of medicine, methods of diagnosis, role of physician and patient and the patient's psyche, prevention and responsibility for health, strengths and limitations.

Eastern Medicine

Key Beliefs

Qi is Life, Qi is heart of medicine. Life and Medicine are one.

Health

A state of well-being in which the body is vital, balanced and adaptive to its environment.

Illness, Sickness, Disease

- Disharmony/imbalance and loss of adaptability (a defect of function/energy)
- Any deviation of the body from its normal or healthy state

Symptoms

Manifestation of the body's attempt to heal itself, therefore, messages, signals of unattended, underlying issues; or signs that something needs balancing.

Causes of Illness

Any action/force, which interferes with the balance and movement of bio-energy: ones constitution, psyche, lifestyle, trauma, environmental stress (nature of human).

Progression of Illness

Four stages of illness from 1) energy imbalances causing 2) functional changes that can initiate 3) a progression of chronic illness preceding 4) pathological changes in tissue.

Personal Responsibility

Key energetic changes are functions of ones psyche and lifestyle so preventing serious illness is primarily self-care.

The Physician

As gardener, assistant: to cultivate life, to help patient get/stay well.

Treatment

Preventing illness by balancing disharmonious energy and counseling lifestyle management.

Science

- Of observation and experimentation, the original science, the ancients understood.
- Einsteinian physics and quantum field mechanics where $E=MC^2$.

Bio-Energy

Must be balanced (rhythmically), free-flowing/circulating, and continually replenished/of sufficient quantity.

Mind-Body

- Mind and body are one, inextricably interconnected. All medicine is psychosomatics.

Iatrogenic Illness (physician caused)

- Virtually non-existent.

Key Limitation

Dependent on harmony with nature, it was not developed to deal with the worst of Western life: overwhelming and unprecedented environmental pollution, iatrogenic illness (physician caused), and consequences of the Western philosophy of individualism and the controlling and defeating nature.

Key Strengths

Prevention, handling functional/chronic illness and self-care: Because it recognizes the key role of lifestyle and the psyche in energetic changes that can progress toward illness.

Western Medicine

Key Beliefs

Humans can control nature. Foreign invader causes illness. Control of symptoms = cure of disease.

Health

Absence of disease, pain, defect, or symptoms of illness (no theory of health).

Illness, Sickness, Disease

- A defect of tissue or structure
- A destructive process with a specific cause and characteristic symptom, a particular disorder.

Symptoms

Manifestation of the disease, therefore, they are disagreeable phenomena to be eliminated or suppressed.

Causes of Illness

A foreign invader, an extraneous force or pathogen: distinct entities with unique causes originating outside the body for every clinical disorder.

Progression of Illness

A progression of a particular disease is noted, but only disorders of form and structure (morphology) are recognized, not progression of functionality into structure.

Personal Responsibility

- Patient's stories are mistrusted and personal conditions considered irrelevant.

The Physician

- As mechanic: to fix what is broken.

Treatment

- Curing named disease and suppressing symptoms through drugs or surgery.

Science

- Of reduction and induction, analytic and controlled science, mechanical.
- Newtonian physics, long ago proved wrong at the cosmic and sub-molecular levels.

Bio-Energy

- Not considered

Mind-Body

- Mind and body are separate and not necessarily connected.

Iatrogenic Illness (physician caused)

- 4th leading cause of death, harms millions.

Key Limitation

Unaware of energy-based physiology (Qi), it therefore cannot detect, classify, measure or alter its effects in its beginning stages of illness. From this flaw stem not only the remaining differences listed above, but the worst consequences of western medicine regularly and inevitably, it harms people.

Key Strengths

- Handling structural defects: trauma and life-threatening illnesses.

Begin with an acknowledgement and prayer:

Thank you Lord for the gift of life . . . I praise you for the promise of health.

I ask you Lord, in Jesus name to use me in service of your Grace. You are my Lord; apart from you, I have no good thing. Thy will be done on earth as it is in heaven, in Jesus name I pray, Amen.

Love & Acceptance of Self

Fill in the blanks with your Name

I love you ________________. I accept you completely.

I know you ________________. You are dear and sweet.

The Promise of Health is your birthright . . .

Call upon me in the day of trouble; I will deliver you, and you will honor me.

—Psalm 50:15 NIV

You have Victory now. Praise Him in spite of everything. In spite of what the doctor says.

Empowerment will come from remembering that divine grace and intelligence will lead you to wellness. When one embraces the reality that God has limitless remedies at His disposal, and realizes the strength of the body's ability to heal, the reward is to proceed with your healing journey, confident and full of promise. This is the promise of health.

Write your current Diagnosis in the first stone.

-----------This line serves as a walled off past----------

Let's move to the present and your good future. Take a moment to realize that the point of diagnosis was merely a brief point in time. A snapshot of what was true in that moment and yet, you live in a body that is always changing at every moment. Your body is changing and healing right now.

Describe your favorite place, the place that brings you joy and peace:

____

____

____

____

____

____

____

____

____

Draw a circle around your description or the name of the place you described above.

This will be your jumping point, your rock on which to stand in joy, fearlessness and gratitude. Standing on this rock, you are already well. Free of worry and fully trusting in God. You are whole, you are healthy, it just has not revealed itself yet.

Write your preferred school of thought (i.e. Western or Eastern Medicine):

____

*Remember it is okay to leave some answers blank as you decide. The answers will come. You may view the empty spaces as having a vast, and unlimited potential for the moment.

Write which Doctor(s) or Hospital(s) you prefer:

Write your feelings associated with these Doctor(s) or Hospital(s):

Write down each treatment option and how long they might take:

How will these treatments effect your quality of life expectations?

Note dates you will get testing done

What outcomes do you expect?

How will you proceed if more time is needed on your healing journey? What steps will you take to get to the desired outcome? Note some alternative ideas, (i.e. what you may choose if current treatments fail):

This is your wellness position where diagnostic tools reveal your wellness.

My Wellness

You can jump ahead in your mind to the wellness positioned stone anytime you are feeling doubt, fear or anxiety about your current health as defined by snapshots in time. That is, imagine yourself completely healed.

False Beliefs Eradicated

Let's take a few minutes to reveal false beliefs and then take the time to re-frame or rewrite those beliefs so they are in line with the truth for us now. We will do this by first completing sentences that are started for you, writing the first thought that comes to your mind. After you read those answers, take some time to look at them and contemplate if you feel they are true sentences. It is my guess that many of the sentences have been completed with negative/false beliefs. We are changing these to positives now, once and for all. Now in the new spaces, fill in the answers with positive and affirming statements. For example, my name is Rhoda and I am good, loving, kind and considerate. I deserve all good things and am blessed with a wonderful character.

There is something wrong with me because

____

I fall short of people's expectations when

____

I am not lovable because

____

I am afraid when

____

I am alone when

____

I am unworthy of forgiveness because

____

Transformed into:

I constantly embrace my whole self.
I embrace all aspects of myself.
I am loved.
I am not afraid.
I am never alone.
I am forgiven.

There is nothing wrong with me because I am wonderfully and woefully made by God. He perfected me through Jesus sacrifice and resurrection.

God gave us a choice. Salvation is there for the taking, if/when you ask. To destroy the separation between you and God say this simple prayer so that He may indwell you: "God, I know I inherited sin, please wash it away. I accept Jesus who died for me as my Lord and Savior, I ask for forgiveness, it is in Jesus name I pray, Amen.

Breaking Ties

One of the first things I was guided to do while ill was to break ties. I can only explain that God directed me to separate myself energetically from many of the people I loved. These were friends and family members I had been "giving to energetically." Although I was intimidated at the process of this type of "letting go", I understood this was a necessary task. Naturally, I had fears about what this could mean for my future relationships with each one of them. I knew this step was necessary for my survival and realized that however I had been in relationship to these people was no longer a healthy choice for me. Instead of hanging on to old ways, I had to grow, accept change. This was necessary for my wholeness. God was making room for a new life and I had to trust in that. As this was a necessary element on my healing path, I share the process with you as a guide if you feel it would benefit your health to do the same. In my case, the outcome of this practice is still unfolding. New relationships have sprung with most of these people that I believe are healthier for both parties. You may also be led to completely sever ties with a certain few.

The process of breaking energetic ties involved these elements:

1. Imagining standing with one of my friends and feeling what it was like to be with them. Contemplating how I felt about them, examining my love for them.
2. Using my mind's eye, looking for the energy that stood between us.
3. Imagining claiming back all energy I gave in relationship to them.
4. Imagining cutting or breaking the energy we shared in relationship to each other.

5. Making the decision to no longer interact energetically with that person in the same way.
6. Allowing myself to become free and clear of my old way of relating.
7. Accepting my aloneness/individuality standing in that space we used to share.

Decision-Making

"A Time for Pause" – take more time when indecision arises. Wait for other possibilities to reveal themselves. If the answer is not clear, it is possible you have not hit on the correct choice or timing at that moment in your healing journey.

How do I make decisions?

____

Possible answers: emotionally, intellectually, logically, intuitively

State your intention(s)

____

Do I blame myself or others for my illness?

____

If so, why?

____

Who must I forgive?

____

Are you afraid?

____

What are you afraid of?

____

What is your highest hope or expectation for the outcome?

____

____

____

____

Do you truly believe this is possible? Yes or No? _______

If No, what or who is in your way?

____

Write a statement regarding any unsupportive person(s), situation(s) or idea(s) that you believe are hindering your healing. Change each statement to a positive statement with a good outcome or belief.

____

____

____

____

____

____

God has promised to provide you all that you need. He is interested in your healing, ask him to help you, guide you, and release all doubt.

Remedy to Rejection of Self

- As God perfected me in Christ, he lifted immense pressure I had placed on myself to be perfect.
- Self-imposed pressure to be perfect may cause oppression and/or rejection of self. This disease-causing psyche may be reversed:

Imagine & Write God's Definition of you when he created you:

____

____

____

Imagine & Write what God sent you here for:

____

____

____

Set Goals for your life!

Write an acknowledgment of what you have already accomplished, things you are proud of, (i.e. character, education, work or family life):

____

____

____

Write down the main things you want to accomplish in your life:

____

____

____

____

____

____

Write a list below of people or things in your life that no longer make you happy:

____

____

____

____

____

____

Conditional Statements

What do I believe?

I am perfect when I

____

____

I will be perfect if I

____

____

Unconditional Statements

The Truth of the Matter:

I am perfect because God made me in his image. I love myself completely as I am today, right now!

Notes:

Developmental Prayer

Dear Lord,

I praise you today, my Holy Father for hearing my prayer. I thank you for my perfect cellular health. I know that in my mother's womb, at the point of conception I was flawless in my development. That each time my cells were divided, they were kept in your perfect light and re-bound together without any imperfections. I know that any trauma that my mother went through during my pregnancy was healed and I was untouched by anything of harm. I was held in nothing but your perfect grace, which endured throughout my first nine-months of development.

At my birth, my mother and I were held in your right hand and all went along with your perfect plan for my health. Each cell had divine intelligence to glorify you and indeed developed perfectly without any hindrance from outside forces. I was unharmed by any vaccination or medicines that were administered at the time of my birth.

Through my infancy you were there to surround me in your likeness. You protected me from any harm and I was healed fully and completely from any childhood accidents or any traumatic event(s).

In my pre-teens I praise you that you oversaw every circumstance and directed my healing even then. You were there to protect and regard my every thought. I ask now that any harm that was done to me on the cellular or emotional and physical level was perfectly healed and I went on to develop into a perfectly healthy adult. I praise you that any trauma or guilt that arose during my adulthood was perfectly and permanently reversed so that my cellular, physical and emotional health was fully restored and the trauma is now null and void.

I praise you now and thank you for reminding me that I am indeed in-filled with the Holy Spirit and that wellness is my birthright. I praise you for allowing my treatment to work perfectly for exactly what it was intended. Thank you for my ultimate healing and restoration to perfection so that I may glorify you. I am restored to perfect health on all levels, spiritually, physically and emotionally. I have received the miracle of acknowledging your awesome ability to form me perfectly in your image. You are the great physician, Jehova Rapha.

In Jesus name I pray, Amen.

Daily Affirmations:

I constantly embrace my whole self.

I do not reject or deny any part of who I am in order to please others.

I am wonderfully and woefully made by God. He perfected me through Jesus sacrifice and resurrection.

I am committed to expressing myself as God made me, in this world.

I am committed to fulfilling my life-purpose.

I strive to deepen my connection with the divine.

I am completely loved and cared for by God.

I am not afraid because God protects me and guides me, making safe passage for me to live out my life.

God is always near, so I am never alone.

I am worthy of forgiveness and I have been forgiven.

Reminder -

Ask each day to be freed from the oppression of illness. Say this simple command. In the name of Jesus I command all roots of illness, infirmity and all roots of anything unhealthy to leave me. You can specify your exact ailment, for example, I command all roots of "Uterine Cancer" to come out of me in the name of Jesus, Amen.

Remember, once you ask, it is given to you!

RESOURCES

Links provided for research and possible inclusion during your healing journey:
http://www.safesolutionsinc.com/cancer.htm

Get information about your tumor (3-5 Year window)
If your cancer is already metastatic or if you have any recurrence you may wish to get more information about your specific cancer. Per request your tumor sample will be sent out to this lab and tested for effective treatments. This is invaluable information if you end up having to get chemotherapy. You decide what you will receive. You also need to decide whether or not you will allow a doctor to plug you into the "standard of care" if it includes a non-effective chemo or other agent for your cancer.

http://www.carislifesciences.com/oncology-target-now

Beck Protocol explains why EMP may be effective in ridding the body of various ailments, viruses, diseases or illness.
http://www.sharinghealth.com/beckprotocol.html

The Protocol Kit –

(1) Electro Magnetic Pulser (EMP), (2) Water Ozonator and (3) colloidal silver maker (called the Silver Pulser on the Sota site). Drink the colloidal silver and ozonated water 1/2 hr. before you use the EMP.

(2) **http://www.sota.com/sota-kits.html**

Medical basics and alternative cancer treatments:

http://www.fourwinds10.net/siterun_data/health/holistic_alternative_medicine/news.php?q=1209404469

BCX Rife

http://www.hymbas.com/RIFEBCXUltra_promo.html

Treatment Centers

Explore the **www.envita.com** website in order to see which treatment options are available to you.

Dr. Johanna Budwig

http://www.budwigcenter.com/about/#.VQ8032Ypcjg

Hippocrates Health Institute
http://hippocratesinst.org/

Read about Hyperbaric Oxygen Therapy:
http://www.californiahyperbarics.com/hbot.html

Obtain imperative information about your health through Testing:

Lab

Genova Diagnostics –
63 Zillicoa St., Ashville, NC 28801

Test:

Chronic Viral Panel #4 includes:

Human Herpes Virus, HHV6, IgG (serum)
EBV Nuclear Antigen, EBNA IgG (serum)
EBV Nuclear Antigen, EBNA IgM (serum)
EBV Early Antigen-Diffuse, EBEA-D IgG (serum)
EBV Viral Capsid Antigen, VCA IgG (serum)
EBV Viral Capsid Antigen, VCA IgM (serum)
CMV, IgG (serum)
CMV, IgM (serum)

Lab

IGenex, Inc.
795 San Antonio Road,
Palo Alto, CA 94303 (800) 832-3200

Test

LYME IgG & IgM Western Blot
Note: be sure all 12 bands are included in test, i.e.: 18, 23-25, 28, 30, 39, 41, 45, 58, 66, 83-93kDa.

Also note: Tests for Lyme other than the Western Blot may yield a high percentage of false negatives

Lab

American Metabolic Laboratories
1818 Sheridan St., Suite 102, Hollywood, FL 33020 – (954) 929-4895

Test

CA Profile (HCG-IRMA, HCG-IMM, HCG-URINE QANT., PHI, GGTP, CEA, DHEA-S, TSH) and Included is PSA if for Men. Although the HCG and PHI are well documented, they are not approved for tumor marker. However, they are indicators, which can be noted, measured and referred to for comparison(s) later.

Lab

Doctor's Data, Inc.
3755 Illinois Ave., St., Charles, IL 60174-2420

Test

Toxic Metals

Aluminum
Antimony
Arsenic
Barium
Beryllium
Bismuth
Cadmium
Cesium
Gadolinium

Lead
Mercury
Nickel
Palladium
Platinum
Tellurium
Thallium
Thorium
Tin
Tungsten
Uranium
Creatinine

Note: Mercury is used in Dental Amalgams (50% by weight). One may consider replacing them with a Composite Dental filling that does not contain any metals.

http://www.icnr.com/articles/mercury-amalgam-toxicity.html

Detox

Infrared Sauna

http://www.overstocksaunas.com/_Precision_Therapy_Portable_Far_Infrared_Sauna_with_Foot_Pad_and_Negative_Ion_-_Large_--SKU_FIRPORTABLELG-BFL.html

Himalayan Salt Bath

http://www.himalayansalt.com/bath-salt.php

Epsom Salt Bath

http://health.howstuffworks.com/skin-care/problems/treating/epsom-salt-baths.htm

Video on Ionized radiation:

http://www.cancer.org/Cancer/CancerCauses/OtherCarcinogens/MedicalTreatments/radiation-exposure-and-cancer

If you want to track your cancer consider Thermography (A safe diagnostic tool), and other safe cancer markers, i.e., the CA Profile mentioned above.

Diagnostic Tests (no ionized radiation):

Thermography

http://naturalhealthcenter.mercola.com/services/thermography.aspx?s_kwcid=TC%7C15735%7Cthermography%7C%7CS%7Cb%7C9483878104&gclid=CJGQkOLQ7KwCFacZQgodUCMJJA

Ultrasound

MRI

Research

PubMed.com

Look for studies in which you are similar to the patients. The more you have in common with the study group, the better you may discern for yourself if this is a desirable choice. If you do not feel confident in your ability to discern the studies, find a friend or family member who is willing to report back what they have discerned.

Importance of Vitamin D daily

http://articles.mercola.com/sites/articles/archive/2012/11/29/unnecessary-melanoma-surgeries.aspx?e_cid=20121129_DNL_US_art_1
http://products.mercola.com/vitamin-d-spray/?e_cid=20121129_DNL_US_YRP_2&source=nl

Colloidal Silver

http://articles.mercola.com/sites/articles/archive/2009/02/07/new-guidelines-released-for-safe-usage-of-colloidal-silver-supplements.aspx

Why Vitamin C works on Cancer
http://www.youtube.com/watch?v=_PI_rKuQWiE&sns=em&noredirect=1

Fulvic Acid

http://www.optimallyorganic.com/Fulvic.htm?gclid=CPGo4O7L7KwCFQhbhwodR3hcMg

Low Dose Naltrexone (LDN)

http://www.lowdosenaltrexone.org/index.htm#How_does_LDN_work_

Recommended Websites:

Natural News
http://naturalnews.com/

Dr. Mercola
http://www.mercola.com/

What are Xenohormones? A group of either naturally occurring or artificially created compounds showing **hormone**-like properties. Xenohormones are frequently implicated in endocrine disruption.

http://www.soap.com/p/natures-way-dim-plus-estrogen-metabolism-caps-61032?site=CA&utm_source=Google&utm_medium=cpc_S&utm_term=SNA-003&utm_campaign=GoogleAW&CAWELAID=1323203373&utm_content=pla&adtype=pla&cagpspn=pla

Immunecare for Candida

http://www.immunecare.co.uk/product/candigest-plus/?gclid=CLrdkLWSkLoCFW9xQgod9V0AiA

Sea Cucumber

Recommended Reading

The 7 Day Mental Diet by Emmet Fox

Knockout by Suzanne Somers

Fire Your Doctor by Andrew Saul

How to Live Longer and Feel Better by Linus Pauling, PhD

Don't Waste Your Cancer by John Piper

The Stupid Diet - The ABC's to Total Health
by J.D. Dr. Dino Prato - Delia Prato

If you wish to make a contribution to others fighting cancer:

Cancer Warrior Inc.
http://cancerwarriorinc.org/

http://micolpaintings.com/

Disclaimer – Micol Sanko is not a doctor and is not recommending or prescribing any specific treatment for any illness. This is a sharing of opinion and resources.

REFERENCES

Zondervan Publishing House. (1987) Amplified Bible (AMP), from biblehub.com

Biblica, Inc. (2011) The Holy Bible, New International Version (NIV); Zondervan: Grand Rapids, Michigan

Crossway Bibles. (2001) The Holy Bible, English Standard Version (ESV), from biblehub.com

Tyndale House Publishers, Inc. (2007) Holy Bible New Living Translation (NLT), Carol Stream, Illinois 60188

World Bible Publishers. (2001) The Holy Bible, King James Version (KJV), Iowa Falls, IA

The Lockman Foundation. (1995) New American Standard Bible Version (NASB) or (NASV), La Habra, CA

Summary Workbook

Quotes here are from these excellent overviews of Eastern and Western medicine:

- *Hammer, pp 3-19, 35-45, 51-61, 383-402*
- *Beinfield & Korngold, pp 3-47, 380-386*
- *Elias & Ketcham, pp xi – xxvi*
- *Kaptchuk, pp 1-33*

http://www.stresssolutions.info/vrs.htm